# ASSIGNMENT DHAKA

*Margaret Riccardelli*

# ASSIGNMENT

# DHAKA

BY

*Margaret Riccardelli*

S & H Publishing, Inc.
Purcellville, Virginia

S & H Publishing, Inc.
P. O. Box 456
Purcellville, VA 20134
www.sandhbooks.com

Ordering Information:
Quantity discounts are available. For details, contact the "Special Sales Department" at the address above or email sales@sandhpublishing.com.

Assignment Dhaka / Margaret Riccardelli
Travel, Biography, Creative Nonfiction, Bangladesh, Dhaka
ISBN 978-1-63320-073-9 Print Edition
ISBN 978-1-63320-074-6 Ebook Edition

## In Memory of my Parents

*Antoinette DeMola Riccardelli*
*and*
*Richard Erasmo Riccardelli*

# Chapter One

# Arrival

Dhaka, Bangladesh
October 1990

"*Baksheesh, baksheesh,*" they cried over and over. All around me the swarm of ragged beggars called as they reached out to me, touching me. Nothing could have prepared me for this, my first glimpse of the people of Bangladesh. It was a scene from an opera of horrors, Dante's worst nightmare. They said other words, but they had no meaning to me. I knew what *baksheesh* meant, though. Each time they said it, they reached out to me and brought their hands to their mouths.

As they crowded around my colleague Carl and me, I thought there must be hundreds of them, but perhaps it just seemed that way. Emaciated, old and young. A rather handsome looking man with brilliant black eyes smiled at me. I felt something poke me and realized it was his arm, or elbow anyway. His hand and wrist were missing.

My stomach turned. Was it the heat? My God, it must be over 100 degrees, and the humidity must be in the high 90s, even in the airport terminal building. I felt as though I couldn't breathe, couldn't get enough air. A shirtless old man came up to me—too close. His chest was covered with sores. Crusty-looking sores that oozed a yellow substance streaked with blood. I was terrified he might touch me. I felt dirty, contaminated. I wanted to scream. But no, I can't do that. I wanted to put on a brave face, to show that I was up to this job. Carl was telling me to look straight ahead, and move forward as fast as I could, but I couldn't take my eyes off the scene around me. Pitifully thin women with shriveled breasts flapping against their rib cages, many carrying naked children. Something was strange about these children. Then I saw it. It was in their eyes. They looked empty. The children didn't smile or cry or show any emotion at all.

Why was it taking so long to walk through the airport terminal? I followed closely behind Mike. We walked slowly. I tried to speed up but soon bumped into Mike. We walked single file, pushing our way through the dense crowd. The filth of the beggars, together with the heat, humidity, and the smell of urine—my God, the smell was overpowering. I stayed as close to Mike as I could, trying to concentrate on the back of his head as he led the way. He seemed to be oblivious to the horror around him. The throng of beggars followed us out to the curb.

We exited the building to a blast of air so hot I thought I might faint. Each deep breath was hot and thick with dust and exhaust fumes. Mike stopped abruptly, and I bumped into him again. He turned to Carl and me and said something, but I couldn't hear because of the noise of the people around us. I wondered why we were just standing there at the curb.

After a few minutes the embassy car drove up and

stopped in front of us. The car air-conditioner was at full blast. Carl followed me into the back seat. Mike sat up front with the driver. I was in the car only seconds when Carl told me not to look. So, of course, I turned to see what he was referring to. The sight was sickening, and I couldn't help moaning. There was a woman tapping on my window. She was holding a naked baby. The woman's arms were skinny, soiled, and wrinkled. Her dirty hair stuck to her bony skull, only partially covered by her sari, like a shroud. Her eyes were sunk deep into their sockets. She put her nose flat up against my window, just inches from my face. She smiled, and I could see her rotted teeth and blood-red stained gums. Then I noticed the baby's eyes and realized he was blind. I somehow couldn't turn away from her. As the car slowly pulled away from the curb, the woman followed us, hands to her mouth now and crying out, "*Baksheesh, baksheesh.*"

# Chapter Two

# The Beginning

That was my first glimpse of Bangladesh. I felt completely overwhelmed and asked myself, "Why don't I just turn around and go back to Washington, D.C.?" Indeed, why didn't I? Stubbornness? Obstinacy? Pride? Oh yes, my old friend, Stubborn Pride. Having dipped my toes into the experience, I was not yet ready to declare defeat and give up. No, I would not show fear, weakness, or vulnerability. It may have been stubborn pride, but I decided I had to see it through, wherever the road led.

* * *

My journey to Bangladesh actually began a few years earlier when I happened to meet an elegant older lady at a business event. She was my mother's age, beautifully dressed in a tailored business suit. When I noticed her, I thought, that is the way I want to be seen, elegantly coiffured and corporate-looking. I could do it.

I had an excellent, well-paying job in the defense industry, one of thousands of executive assistants with perfectly satisfying careers working for high-ranking retired Air Force colonels. I could have happily enjoyed that job for the remainder of my working life, but my new friend Lillian had stirred up something in me.

Some people are born travelers or perhaps with just an insatiable curiosity about the world and its people. Surely, I must be one of them. I remembered seeing the photos of faraway, exotic places in *National Geographic* magazines when I was growing up in Brooklyn, New York. Temples in Nepal, yurts in Mongolia, and ryokans in the Japanese countryside—I yearned to see these enchanting places. As a child in school, the nuns often accused me of daydreaming. They were right. I was traveling to faraway places in my busy imagination. Hearing Lillian and her friends speak of these destinations reawakened that yearning for travel and adventure.

At twenty-one I started in my first airline job with Alitalia airlines. In those days, once you were employed for a year, you were eligible for travel benefits. After a year on the job, I went to Rome and sent my office a letter of resignation. I rented a room with Signorina Perlini, Miss Little Pearls. For a while I was a runway model for Fabianna, one of Rome's famous fashion designers of Italian knit clothing. Of course, I fell in love and Roberto and I traveled all over Italy and even spent a lovely vacation on the volcanic island of Stromboli. My beautiful year in Italy, and the romance, ended on a sweet note and I returned to the States and my childhood home in Brooklyn.

Fortunately, I immediately went to work for Air Canada, and continued in the airline industry for several more years. I flew around the world a few times. I left the airline industry when I married, a marriage that sadly ended within ten years. After my marriage ended,

I built a new life for myself with a satisfying career. My traveling years were a lovely memory that I rarely talked about. They seemed a lifetime away.

Then I met Lillian and she often talked about her travels. Over coffee one day, I learned that she had a little jewelry business. She traveled abroad on vacation, bought beautiful jewelry, and then sold it at her twice-yearly house parties. She invited me to one of her house parties, and I met many more of her interesting friends. They were all well-traveled and elegantly dressed—some married, some widowed, and some single. I felt comfortable with them, and we often talked of places we had traveled to, although none of the places where I had vacationed were anywhere near as exotic as where she and her friends had lived and worked, like Teheran, Buenos Aires, and Cairo. My career in the airline industry had afforded me the opportunity to do a fair bit of traveling, but this was different.

"Where did you work? What did you do?" I asked one day, so very intrigued and practical.

"We were Foreign Service secretaries. We worked in American embassies around the world," they replied.

"Oh!" I was completely captivated by their answer. "That sounds so interesting." I thought of the first time I went to Italy. I was with my parents who were returning to Italy to visit family after immigrating thirty-five years before. We were walking along the Via Veneto when we saw the American flag flying over the U.S. Embassy. My guidebook noted it was the palace of the former Queen of Italy, Margaret of Savoy. I imagined myself working there, although I had no notion of what embassies did.

But here I was listening to my friends talk about

living overseas and working at an American Embassy. It wasn't such an unattainable concept. Maybe it was within my reach after all.

Helen said, "There would be an extensive background check; you would need to qualify for a Top Secret clearance." Working in the defense industry, I already had a Secret clearance. But a Top Secret clearance sounded so sexy and CIA-ish. My imagination began running wild. Could I do this? What if I did? Would they ask me to be a spy like James Bond? It sounded thrilling and maybe a bit scary. All I focused on was that I would live overseas and work in an American Embassy.

Excited now, I asked my new friends, "Do you think they would hire someone like me?" At forty-five years old, I often thought life was passing me by and considered myself over-the-hill regarding adventure. Lillian's friend Helen replied, "Of course they would. Lillian, let's bring her to meet Peggy."

Their friend Peggy was finishing her Foreign Service career and doing her final assignment in the Human Resource Office as a recruiter for the Foreign Service. Peggy had lived and raised her daughter in Teheran while on assignment there.

Within a few days, I met Lillian and Helen at the entrance to the main State Department building in Washington, D.C. They took me to see Peggy. They must have called her for an appointment because she had a packet of forms ready to give me and took my fingerprints. Before I knew it, I was on my way.

At home I glanced over the material I'd received earlier that day from the State Department. It included a lengthy employment application as well as the FBI questionnaire. I decided to save it and devote a full Saturday to completing all the forms.

Three hours into the forms the following Saturday and I thought I would never get through them. I called my sister, Mary Ann.

"I can't do this. They want to know everything about me, where I ever lived and what countries I have visited. I don't remember."

"Take a deep breath," my practical sister instructed. "Just do the best you can and then let the chips fall where they may."

I wrote this sentence on the folder, "Let the chips fall where they may."

It took another four hours to complete the paperwork, hoping I had listed all the countries I had traveled to in my airline career. When I finished, I was exhausted, but I wrapped it up and decided I had done my best. The outcome was out of my hands. Now all I could do was wait for the chips to start falling.

Yes, I applied to the Foreign Service on kind of a whim, not knowing exactly what it was all about, except what Lillian and her friends had told me. I enthusiastically went along as they mentored me through the rather cumbersome application process: eighteen months of interviews, tests, and medical examinations, as well as that extensive investigation by the FBI. I filled out and signed endless documents sent to me and showed up on time for all the interviews, and then one day…voila!

* * *

I received a call from the Human Resource Office of the U.S. Department of State and heard the magic words.

"I am pleased," (I realized I was holding my breath.) "to inform you that you have been accepted into the American Foreign Service." I exhaled!

"Ah, oh, where am I going?" I asked breathlessly.

"You must accept the appointment first. Do you recall signing a document that asked you if you would go anywhere the U.S. government sent you?"

"Yes," I replied. Of the hundreds of papers I'd signed, I actually did remember that one.

"What it means is that you must first accept the appointment."

I hesitated for barely a moment because there was one country in the world that I never wanted to go to again.

"I accept," I replied quickly, taking a chance that she would not mention that one country. After several visits to Japan I wasn't interested in returning there when I had the whole world to see.

"Welcome to the American Foreign Service," she replied.

"In a few weeks you will receive a call from your assignments officer advising you where you have been assigned."

"Okay," I replied. "Thank you. Goodbye."

I called my sister Mary Ann immediately. "I'm in! State Department just called me. I'm in!" We both screamed in glee.

"You're just like a cat, Marg. No matter how you fall you always land on your feet." Mary Ann said. "Congratulations!" We laughed.

I called my folks and several friends. They all had the same question, "Where are you going?"

Well, that was it. I was in. My next step was to contain my curiosity and excitement and wait for the next call from the State Department. Yikes, I thought. Three weeks! The suspense! The tension! With every phone call, my heart stopped. Was this it?

Precisely three weeks later, a different Human Resource representative called. Holding my breath, I waited. With a smile in her voice she said, "Congratulations, you have been assigned to Dhaka." There was a pause the length of a breath, and then she said Bangladesh. I was glad she said where it was because I had no idea and was too embarrassed to ask her. Hearing the country name, I immediately thought of the Beatles.

When I returned home that evening, I quickly pulled out my big *National Geographic World Atlas* and looked for Bangladesh. To the right of India and to the left of Burma. Curry. Silk saris. Ah, the Bengal Sea—Bengal tigers—I was slowly forming a picture. My cousin had a close friend who was from Bangladesh. I ate Indian food and liked it. I once knew a girl from Burma (next to Bangladesh) and recalled she was lovely and spoke English with an elegant British accent. I searched for my Beatles record album, *Concert for Bangladesh.* On the cover was a photo of a child. Were those flies on her mouth? But she was such a beautiful child, and that was a very long time ago. Wasn't it?

* * *

Over the next several weeks there were many calls with instructions on where to report for work, new forms to complete, and appointments to schedule. The enormity of what I needed to do before my new career started began to sink in. I had two months before I would begin two months of intensive training at the Foreign Service Institute, the training center for the American diplomatic corps.

Four months seemed a sufficient amount of time. In my usual meticulous way, I began to make a to-do list in a notebook that I kept with me at all times. Whenever I thought of something, I would quickly jot it down. As the days went by, the items on the list multiplied instead of diminished. In fact, the list seemed to grow by the minute. Four months was beginning to sound like a frighteningly short period of time to prepare for such a move. I sensed the urgency. I wanted to have all the tasks completed before I started my training. What to do with my condo? What to do with my car? Questions, questions, questions. Can I drive in Bangladesh? *Should* I drive in Bangladesh? The library was not much help, as there was not a lot of information available about Bangladesh. India would have to be my guide. How different could it be from India?

Fortunately, I soon began receiving mounds of information from my assignment officer at State Department. It included recommendations on all kinds of things, from personal care items and clothes to how to stay healthy in a third-world country. And the odd recommendation that I prepare a legal last will and testament. I had traveled to third-world countries before, so I knew what that meant, but I usually stayed in modern hotels and ate in recommended restaurants. I pored over the material that answered some of my questions.

A friend introduced me to Marie, who was in the

Foreign Service and living in Washington D.C., preparing for her next assignment to Hong Kong. Wow—Hong Kong! She was enormously helpful to me and we arranged to meet up in Bangkok when we were both settled, her in Hong Kong and me in Dhaka. This was sounding more and more exciting to me, and I couldn't wait. I also spoke with former Peace Corps volunteers, who generously offered more suggestions. I learned that fruits and vegetables needed to be soaked in a solution of water, soap, and bleach. Question: how do I rinse the food off after they have soaked in the soap and bleach? Do I use contaminated water? Of course not! Answers to questions produced more questions. I'll worry about that later, I thought.

I joined the Department of State Federal Credit Union so I could easily handle finances overseas. Every American Embassy overseas has a cashier's office where you can cash a check and get local currency. There is also a mailroom that sells U.S. stamps and that will arrange shipments though the American postal system.

Each day after work, I tore through my apartment sorting my belongings into piles labeled "storage," "bring," and "dump." The piles shifted as I asked myself, do I really need this, or, should I take that? As I told friends what I was doing, they offered more advice and ideas on the best body lotion, mosquito repellent, or pesticide. When I saw a discount ad for toothpaste or pasta, I bought enough to last for two years, running up staggering credit card balances. It was a daunting task.

I hired a property manager who would find tenants for my condo, take care of all the documentation, and follow up with the tenants while I was gone. My brother offered to buy my car. Definitely, I should not drive in Bangladesh.

At the end of two months, most of the items on my to-do list had been crossed off. Miraculously, I was ready.

* * *

I arrived early for my first day of orientation. There were about a hundred people in the entry-level group—Foreign Service specialists in all categories; financial, general services, medical, information technology, and security among them. I was one of about twenty in the new class of Foreign Service secretaries. Each of us stood up proudly that first day and announced our names and where we were assigned: London, Tokyo, Rome, Beijing, Buenos Aires, Dhaka. On and on, we introduced ourselves.

We were given piles of information about living overseas, staying safe and how to behave. The dos and don'ts of diplomatic protocol. We were prompted on how to formally address ambassadors. We had photos taken for our Diplomatic Passports and forms to complete and present to our respective foreign ministry upon arrival. We received a list of inoculations required for the country where we were assigned and made appointments with the medical office. There were suggestions on spousal employment and schools for children. I learned in the orientation program that there were several families joining the Foreign Service. A few were called tandem couples, husband and wife in different Foreign Service jobs traveling overseas together.

After three weeks of orientation, the secretaries

broke away from the main group to start specialized training. For three more intense weeks, we focused on managing an embassy front office, working in a secure area called a *skiff*. We learned about handling classified documents, codes, how to work a variety of safes and locks, and too many communication formats. We even received "violations" if we improperly handled pretend classified information, just as we would in an actual embassy office. Just an aside, each evening at embassies worldwide, a U.S. Marine checks to be sure safes are secure and the embassy in lockdown. If classified information is found unsecured, the last person to leave the office—usually the secretary—receives a violation. Three violations could mean dismissal from the Foreign Service.

After the training, we were expected to know our job, but I didn't feel very confident and was apprehensive. Yet I continued onward. One more additional week of training did the trick; we were assigned to an office at the main State Department building downtown to get a bit of on-the-job experience.

Training complete, bags packed but not yet closed, there were many dinner parties to say goodbye to family and friends. Still running on some kind of energy I had not known I possessed, the day of my swearing-in arrived.

My mother came down from New Jersey for the official ceremony in the elaborately decorated Benjamin Franklin diplomatic ceremonial room of the State Department. As family and friends of the new graduates entered the impressive room, many looked around in awe. This was the room where bilateral and multilateral treaties were signed and heads of state met. It was an important event.

I was dressed in a new suit I bought for the event. I had a new hairdo and polished nails as I stood proudly with my colleagues. You could feel the excitement. There were several speeches by State Department principals who spoke to us as members of the Foreign Service, explaining that we were to be the face of America to the world. Secretary of State James A. Baker was then introduced to deliver the oath. We all stood proudly and swore that we would go anywhere and do anything for the United States of America. I admit that I was emotional and had tears in my eyes. I thought of my parents who were both farmers in Italy before they came to America as teenagers. I'm sure it was poignant for my mother as well, although when we met after the ceremony, she was preoccupied trying to figure out how on earth they cleaned the many sparkling chandeliers.

My last four days were with my family, attending even more emotional farewell parties. I wondered how my nieces would change in two years. How would I change? I didn't sleep the night before I left my parent's house in South Jersey. We drove to Valley Stream, Long Island, for yet another farewell event, this one with more aunts, uncles, and cousins. My Uncle Frank drove my parents and me to Kennedy Airport. At the check-in counter I proudly presented my diplomatic passport to the agent. My parents walked me to the departure gate. Tears and one last kiss, my mother handed me something in a brown paper bag.

I boarded the plane and secured my safety belt. Within a few minutes, the plane took off. Up into the clouds, the plane climbed and soon leveled off, heading for the distant horizon and my future. I remembered the bag my mother handed me at the last moment and opened it. It was the most delicious chicken parmesan sandwich on hard crusted Italian bread with sesame seeds I ever had. My favorite.

A couple glasses of red wine and the chicken sandwich, along with the lull of the aircraft motor, put me into a deep, restless sleep. I was so exhausted from the last several months that when sleep finally came, I didn't fight it. I sank down into my seat, pulled the blankets over me, and slept.

I had wild, bizarre dreams of headless Argentinian horsemen. In my dream I could see the coarse, black stitching on their shoulders where their heads had once been. They were famous for their daring horsemanship, jumping from one side of the horse to the other in a fast gallop. As they raced around the track, the mud and manure splashed my face and clothes. I rushed into a nearby building, a rowdy bar where more of the horsemen gathered. When they saw me, they rushed toward me. They came closer and closer until, frightened, I began to run. My shoes sank into mud and manure up to my ankles. One of the riders overtook me, grabbed my arm, and pulled me to him. He smelled of dirt and sweat, and I struggled to get away. I awoke to the flight attendant tapping my shoulder and asking me if I would like breakfast. We were about an hour out of London.

It was a disturbing dream, yet I wanted to remember it for some reason. I jotted down the details in my notebook. It was graphic and incredibly bizarre. I had never been to Argentina and had never been to any racetrack. Where do dreams come from? I wrote down as much of the dream as I could in as much detail as possible. After a while my anxiety dissipated.

The long flight from London to Bombay was uneventful. At the suggestion of the State Department's travel agent, I paid for an upgraded seat and was glad I did. The seats were comfortable, and the food was delicious. I arrived in Bombay feeling relaxed and refreshed. While waiting for the Biman Bangladesh Airlines flight into Dhaka, I met a colleague, the only other Westerner waiting for the flight. Carl introduced himself to me. He was a junior officer, also assigned to the economic/commercial section. As we walked through the Bombay airport terminal and waited for our connecting flight, we chatted comfortably. Carl grew up in the Swedish Foreign Service. His father was on a U.S. assignment when he met and married Carl's American mother. She encouraged Carl to join the American diplomatic corps. We were both on our first assignment.

As we walked along the corridors of the Bombay airport terminal, we were both surprised to see so many beggars, many holding young babies who were thin and sickly. There were no shops to speak of, except for a few stalls selling mostly cheap, fragile souvenirs. The bathrooms were free of trash but had a strong smell of old urine.

We changed our flight seats so we could sit together for the two-hour flight into Dhaka. There were so few people on the flight from Bombay to Dhaka that Carl and I were put in the first-class section. When our flight was announced, we boarded the plane. I noticed a roach that must have been trapped behind the "Exit" sign. It was darting from the "T" to the "I" and then back to the "T" again before disappearing behind the "E." Talking with Carl and watching the roach made the flight go quickly.

In no time at all, we were flying over what looked like an endless body of water with the tops of trees and houses peeking through. There were many people perched on top of the flat-roofed houses. The plane dipped low and circled the city before it slowly began its descent. We landed smoothly in a large puddle of water with a reflection of the blue cloudless sky.

As soon as the seatbelt sign was turned off, the flight attendant opened the aircraft door. We quickly gathered our things and exited the plane before the other passengers. Mike, our new boss, was right there at the gate to greet us and introduce himself. He shook our hands in a friendly and casual welcome.

"Okay, let's go. Follow me," Mike said, and we followed him to the baggage claim area. He introduced us to the embassy expediter who would collect our bags for us and get our passports stamped. As we waited, we stood talking with Mike.

# Chapter Three

# Welcome to Bangladesh

Mike was the economic minister at our embassy in Dhaka. We chatted comfortably as we waited for our luggage in the secure part of the airport. After our bags were collected and passports stamped, we followed Mike out of the secure area, into the arrival terminal, and into the shocking and horrifying throng of beggars. Why hadn't he warned us? I learned later that Mike was what the State Department called a "South Asia hand," meaning most of his career was spent in these poor countries of South and Southeastern Asia. I believe he just got used to seeing the extreme level of poverty and it no longer shocked him.

Driving from the airport through the streets of Dhaka, Mike and Carl talked while I remained silent, still feeling overwhelmed by the airport experience. During the half-hour drive, we passed people walking in twos and threes, sidewalk vendors selling fried snacks, broken-down and mildewed shacks of all sorts, packs of roaming dogs with patchy fur, goats, and the odd cow. There were hundreds of rickshaws, baby taxis (small motorized rickshaws), and dilapidated buses chugging along filled with people and with still more people perched on top. Buses and cars honked their horns, rickshaws rang their bells, children played—the noise was deafening. Yet there were people sleeping on collapsed cardboard boxes along the dusty streets or sleeping in the dirt.

Growing up the child of immigrant parents in New York, I thought I had an idea of what poor meant. Once I started traveling, I downgraded my definition a step or two. Yet, nothing in my experience could have prepared me for the level of poverty that now surrounded me. Many of the broken-down shacks were built attached to the high brick walls of palatial estates, and the contrast made the poverty even more stark.

The embassy car stopped in front of a gate in a residential neighborhood. Within moments, a guard in a wrinkled uniform opened the gates and motioned for us to drive forward. We stopped in front of an open two-car garage. It was the carport of a two-story building. The building had a side entrance and Carl and I followed Mike as he opened the door. Together we walked up the stairs. Mike opened a door on the second floor, and we entered a freezing cold, fully furnished apartment.

"This is your apartment." Mike said as he handed me the keys. "Welcome to Bangladesh."

Just like that, I was presented with this huge apartment that seemed to go on and on forever as we walked through four bedrooms, three bathrooms, a very large formal dining room, suitable for an important conference or dinner party, and a large living room. Beyond the living room, there was a large balcony that ran the length of the house overlooking the street. The apartment was furnished with new, matching furniture.

The dining room had twelve chairs around a large table. The living room had several sofas, many chairs of various kinds, and accompanying tables and lamps. The large master bedroom had a queen-sized bed, neatly made up. As we walked through the kitchen, I could see a coffee pot and tea kettle on the counter. Mike picked up a piece of paper and as we walked through to the door, gave it to me.

"Here's a note for you."

"Why don't you settle in for a while, and I'll pick you up about six thirty?"

"Okay, Mike," I responded. "Thank you." He and Carl left me alone in the apartment. It was about one in the afternoon.

I read the note as I walked back into the kitchen.

"Dear Margaret,

Welcome to Bangladesh!

The water in the big tank on the counter has been boiled for the recommended 20 minutes of rolling boil and is now potable. I left a bit of food in the fridge in case you're hungry. See you next week.

Diane, your social sponsor."

Who is Diane, and what is a social sponsor? I had no idea, but I was appreciative of the fresh water. I was thirsty. The first cabinet I opened had glasses and dishes.

I looked in the fridge and found a Pyrex dish of roasted chicken and vegetables. I thought, am I dreaming? This incredible apartment and lovely dinner. It's just like a fairy tale.

I couldn't think any more and felt bone tired.

I lay on the bed and stared at the ceiling, snuggling deep into the warm blankets. I remained that way for several hours and must have dozed a bit. I dreamed but didn't remember about what. It was a restless dream, though. I heard a phone ring somewhere in the apartment but didn't move from that position.

I got up about five thirty and opened my suitcases. The embassy expediter had carried them into the bedroom when we arrived, and they were lined up along the wall.

I was downstairs waiting in the driveway at six thirty when Mike arrived in his personal car. He had a private driver who was also his manservant. Carl was already in the back seat.

"Good evening," I said to no one in particular.

"I hope you got a bit of rest," Mike asked.

There was small talk as we drove to the American Club, just a few blocks away.

Mike showed his club pass to the guard who opened the gate. We walked along a garden path of manicured flower beds and lush lawn. The American Club was a shabby building, mildewed and suspiciously unclean. Mike, Carl, and I were shown to a table and joined a group of people. We were all introduced by name and by which embassy department we worked in. Remembering all these new names was certainly going to be a challenge.

"Welcome to Dhaka," they said.

"Thank you," I said and smiled.

We had drinks. Gin and tonic seemed to be popular, so I ordered one. Most of the group ordered lobster, and I was surprised they trusted eating shellfish here. No one asked me how I liked Dhaka. I wondered what I would have said if they did. Dinner was served, but I couldn't eat much. I tossed some bits of rice and chicken around my plate.

After the welcome-aboard dinner at the American Club, we all gathered for an after-dinner drink at Pearl and Aaron's house. Pearl was a beautiful Bangladeshi woman who had married, at the age of nineteen, a former American Peace Corps volunteer. After Aaron's Peace Corps tour ended, he returned to Bangladesh and found Pearl. They married and traveled the world together in the course of Aaron's long Foreign Service career. Their assignment to Dhaka was his final overseas assignment. Pearl was one of those Bangladeshis with a charming British accent, obviously raised in privilege in this desperately poor country.

After so many hours of flying, I felt dead on my feet and soon nodded off mid-sentence. It was well after ten o'clock by the time Mike dropped me off at my apartment.

Finally alone in my vast apartment, I walked from room to room turning on every light I could find. Then I quickly undressed and fell onto the bed. My body ached, but I no longer had the strength to get up and get an aspirin. I had planned my arrival for a Thursday so I would have the weekend to relax and settle in slowly after the long flight. The work schedule in Islamic countries is Sunday through Thursday. Exhausted, I fell asleep quickly.

I slept erratically, waking up several times. Every noise in the house was scary and I woke, wondering where it was coming from. About three in the morning, I awoke thirsty so went into the kitchen for a glass of water. At first I didn't notice it, but as my eyes focused, I saw the cockroach. It was the biggest roach I had ever seen in my life! It was the size of my fist with long antennae. I didn't know what to do. It was too big for me to kill. I was afraid it would bite me. I ran downstairs crying and woke up the guard at our gate. With tears running down my face, I somehow made him understand that he needed to follow me upstairs. When he saw the roach, he grabbed a small pot on the side of the sink and whacked the damn thing, not once but four or five times. I think it scared him as well. After the guard left, I collapsed on the bed in tears and after some time fell into a restless sleep.

# Chapter Four

# To the Market

I was awakened in the early morning to the melodic sound of the first call to prayer at dawn. "Allahu Akbar" rang out from several mosques in the neighborhood.

Audrey, a colleague who had arrived in Bangladesh a month prior to me and whom I had met in Washington, D.C., came by my apartment early on that first Friday morning. We had made the arrangements in Washington while in training, since we were both assigned to Dhaka. It was her first Foreign Service assignment, too. I was anxious to see her and tell her how I was feeling and ask her how she was taking it all in. Instead, Audrey arrived full of enthusiasm and seemed anxious to show me the city. When we met in Washington, she wasn't exactly looking forward to this assignment. Seeing her so excited now, happy, and dare I say cheerful, I was puzzled how she had settled in so quickly. I didn't reveal my horror from the airport experience and didn't mention the gigantic cockroach that greeted me the night before. I finished dressing and went along with her to the market in the embassy car she had hired for a few hours.

As soon as the big American car pulled up to the

market area, about a dozen children ran toward the car. "Madam, madam," they cried. They had their hands outstretched and said that word again and again, *baksheesh.* Audrey tapped about four of them on the head, one by one. As she did, she said, "carry person." Then the next child, "protector." Several others joined our entourage, following us closely.

The local shopping area was a little more than half a mile from my house. It was a two-story shopping center, dilapidated and heavily mildewed. On the first floor was a large indoor marketplace set up with all the vegetable vendors clustered in one area, the rice vendors clustered in another corner, the spice vendors in another, and so on, all on a pounded dirt floor splattered here and there with red phlegm. It was dimly lit with a few lightbulbs dangling from long cords attached to wires high above.

Most of the customers were Bangladeshis. Few Europeans or other non-Bangladeshis would do their own shopping. But Audrey told me I should familiarize myself with the prices, although I couldn't make heads or tails out of the currency yet. I was accustomed to the kilo-to-pound ratio already. Audrey introduced me to her favorite vendors, telling me that they would not cheat me. They in turn responded, "Good prices." I was learning quickly and keeping mental notes on all her suggestions.

The children Audrey designated as our "carry persons and protectors," along with several other children and beggars followed us. She explained to me it was a good idea to always keep the children close to me in the shopping areas or the beggars would continually harass me.

I bought carrots, string beans, onions, and tomatoes. They were all beautifully displayed and looked fresh and delicious. As I handed the produce bags to my carry person, the little boy looked up at me with the most incredible hazel eyes. My heart melted. He was so beautiful and yet heartbreakingly dressed in filthy rags. His hair was a dirty and tangled mess of black curls. He looked straight into my eyes and smiled. I smiled back at him, and he responded by giggling. I reacted by laughing, which made him laugh even more. The other children began laughing, too. By this time Audrey began to laugh. It was an extraordinary experience. Spontaneous joy in an unexpected setting.

All the produce was plump and ripe, and there was an abundance of it. No food shortage here, I thought. I bought a kilo of rice, and to this day I'm not sure exactly what type of rice I bought. Rice is rice, right? There was a selection of perhaps ten to twenty different kinds of rice to choose from. The last item on my list was milk. Audrey reminded me that it wasn't pasteurized and had to be boiled, something to do later that day. The comment reminded me that I needed to buy bleach as well, since all the fruit and vegetables needed to be soaked in a solution of bleach and water to kill any bacteria.

Silently, I asked myself, “Will I survive this?”

With the children following us, we walked around the shopping center on a little tour, and Audrey identified the different shops. Upstairs were art stores offering lovely frames and exciting, creative, original art that was quite good. Shoemakers displayed custom-made shoes to order in a variety of leathers and colors.

There were several antique vendors, and we walked through those shops. I bought a few brass items that Audrey bargained and paid for, as I hadn't changed any money yet. There were several dressmakers to hire and beautiful, colorful fabric for sale. Audrey told me I could bring a picture of a dress and they would make it for me. There were sari vendors and little notion shops. All manner of food, clothing, and trinkets could be bought in this one shopping center. Also, it was open 24 hours a day. There was even a vendor selling American products, although Audrey told me street people would go through our trash and sell the containers to storeowners, who would then fill the containers with strange concoctions. Better to buy name brands at our commissary. The children carried our bags to the waiting embassy driver, and Audrey gave them a few coins each.

"Are you ready to interview maids yet?" Audrey asked me.

"I would rather not hire one," I said. Honestly, I had no idea what the maid would do. Living alone and neat by nature, it seemed to me a maid would be an unnecessary expense. Audrey didn't offer any advice but had an odd smile on her face when I told her.

"I'll ask you again in a few days," she said.

We drove around our neighborhood and stopped at a clothing store. I bought a lovely *salwar kameez* (tunic top and matching pants) in a bright gold, cotton fabric. Audrey loaned me the money. There were several other pretty items that I was sure I couldn't live without. We stopped at the American Club for lunch before continuing the tour.

By the time we returned to my house a few hours

later, I was completely exhausted. Audrey said I should rest and that she would pick me up at seven o'clock that evening. We were invited to dinner at the house of another colleague, Ellen. I made myself a cup of tea and put a couple drops of milk in it, thinking a little wouldn't kill me. I felt awfully dirty and decided to take a shower. While washing my face, I sniffed a bit of warm water because my nose was stuffed up. Out came black soot.

"What on earth..." I said out loud to the shower head.

God only knows what I breathed in if this is what came out of my nose.

* * *

Audrey picked me up at seven o'clock as promised. She had hired an embassy driver to take us to Ellen's house, just a few blocks from mine. It seemed there was an unlimited supply of embassy cars available to rent for twenty-five cents a mile, with the embassy billing us once a month. Actually, the embassy had about five cars in total, and the embassy drivers on staff often volunteered to be on call to embassy staff. We, in turn, tipped them generously, which far exceeded their wages. Driving in Dhaka was not recommended and could be hazardous to one's health, if not life itself.

Ellen lived in a large house surrounded by a high red brick wall enclosing lush and flowering gardens. The driver drove right up to the gate, and within moments the guard came running out, and we proceeded up to the entrance. Ellen's maid, Feroza, waited at the open door.

Ellen was a twenty plus year veteran of the Foreign Service and the ambassador's secretary. Her home was a museum of her life and career. There were magnificent

Russian icons on the walls and exquisite hand painted Russian enamel boxes on every table. There was a large box on the coffee table next to me that was painted with a scene of a troika driven by a team of galloping white stallions. Lush Asian silk carpets covered the floors. Several large African masks took up an entire wall in the sitting room. No paper plates here: she had china from Thailand, woven trays from East Africa, and lovely glassware from Egypt. Curio cabinets custom-made in Thailand were filled with handmade Russian chess sets, one more unique than the next. It was clear which furniture was embassy-provided, as it was exactly like mine.

I was introduced to an amazing group of women from the American Embassy, British Embassy, and Australian High Commission. The conversation was lively and interesting, and I felt that I had entered a world I had dreamed of all my life. They wanted to know where I was from in the States and why I joined the Foreign Service. I learned that everyone except Audrey had served in many places, some glamorous and some not. There was a lot of laughter. The food was delicious and Middle Eastern. Ellen had brought all her spices from her previous assignment in Amman, Jordan. The drinks were plentiful, and just about everyone was drinking gin and tonics. That seemed to be the drink of South Asia.

Barbara, Susan, Francine—one by one I met them, and they all seemed so settled into life in Dhaka. At one point, Barbara leaned over to me and whispered, "You'll get used to it."

Wow, I guess my face showed my emotions, and

frankly I was embarrassed. I took a deep breath and corrected my expression.

Audrey and I were the only two who were on their first tour of duty. Almost without exception, the others talked about their prior assignments or the things their maids or manservants had done that puzzled them. There was much talk of where to buy this or that, as well as good humor and laughter.

I also met my downstairs neighbor, Eve, another long-time Foreign Service person. When we were introduced, she said, "You poor dear. You look as though you could use a cappuccino." Apparently, I hadn't corrected my expression quite enough. She suggested that I be ready by eleven the following morning for a day out with her, and I readily accepted.

An embassy car picked up Audrey and me at about eleven that evening. By the time I got to bed, I was more than tipsy, and the room was spinning. I fell into a deep sleep with the mental note that I would have to curb my enjoyment of gin and tonics in the future. I slept soundly and peacefully through the night for the first time in several nights and again woke to the sound of the muezzin, calling the faithful to prayer. I realized there must be several mosques nearby because they were not in synch, but rather echoed the prayer throughout the neighborhood.

# Chapter Five

# Madam Upstairs & Madam Downstairs

## Saturday Morning

I was ready at eleven o'clock when I heard the knock at my door. Francis, Eve's manservant, was wearing a *lungi* (ankle-length, wrap-around cloth) with a clean, white, freshly ironed shirt.

He said, "Madam downstairs waiting."

Was it my imagination or did he bow? I thought he said that the madam is downstairs waiting, but I learned later that he didn't say that at all.

"All right," I said. "Tell her I'm on my way."

Eve was waiting in the hired embassy car. The drive to downtown Dhaka took almost an hour in the crowded streets. We passed a cart piled high with…something.

"What do you suppose that is?" I asked my new neighbor.

"Hemp," Eve replied matter-of-factly, as though it was not unusual at all to see a rickshaw pedaled by a skinny little fellow carrying a bundle of hemp four or five times his size.

The traffic was stop-and-go the entire way, and our driver calmly kept up with the symphony of rickshaw bells and automobile horns. The sights along the way were of old buildings, moldy from centuries in the country's high humidity that only enhanced the magnificent architecture dating from the last three hundred years of British rule. There were also makeshift structures, haphazardly nailed together, with families squatting outside cooking their midday meals and many others sleeping on the streets. Beggars were everywhere. We passed a kind of commercial area where we saw one man picking another man's ears with some kind of long wooden gadget. Barbers were shaving men or cutting their hair, while other customers squatted nearby picking their noses. There was a long row of men with old manual typewriters, some typing and some with customers waiting. Much of life here was lived on the streets.

We passed several construction sights and I noticed they all included a pile of red bricks and seated on the very top of the pile was usually a pitifully thin woman with a hammer breaking the bricks into pebble size pieces.

Men were squatting in the middle of the roundabouts with traffic speeding by. I asked Eve what they were doing in the middle of the road.

"They're peeing," she responded, again matter-of-factly. "Here the men squat when they pee, and the women just stand over the open sewer that runs along the street."

"Oh," I said. "Okay." That's all I could say. It did explain the pervasive odor.

Eve seemed to know a lot of things about the country, so I asked her what the red phlegm was on the streets. She told me it was betel nut and paan, a slightly narcotic betel nut leaf wrapped around an areca nut with a dash of lime, placed in the cheek and slowly chewed by both males and females all over South Asia. It induces saliva, which is then spit out. Initially, the gums and tongue become beet red, but eventually, it produces a heavy black tar that coats the teeth, causing them to loosen and fall out. That was what was so frightening at the airport—hundreds of people crowding around me with their bright red mouths and rotted teeth.

Eve and I chatted easily on the drive and we got to know each other a bit. She told me that Francis called me Madam Upstairs, so she decided to do the same. I, in turn, called her Madam Downstairs, and we laughed. This was her final tour of duty, and she was looking forward to going home to California. She recited her address including her zip code. That's how she said it: as of such and such a date, I will be at whatever avenue in whatever hometown. Traveling the world for over 30 years, she was done. No second thoughts.

I learned that she was in the bombing of the Marine Corps barracks in Lebanon in 1983. Several of her friends had died, and she was evacuated soon after. All her possessions were lost.

"Evacuations are like that," she said. "They are sudden and usually directly from the embassy." She suggested that I leave all my jewelry and important documents in a safe in my office so that if an evacuation was declared, I could just pick it up and go.

"Also, I recommend you keep several hundred dollars in small bills in both local and U.S. currency in one easy-to-carry package." Perhaps a premonition, I recognized that as a valuable piece of Foreign Service advice.

* * *

We finally arrived at the Sonargaon Hotel in downtown Dhaka. Their elegantly dressed doorman opened the car door, and as I stepped into the lobby, I suddenly felt I had entered another world. Bangladesh disappeared. The Sonargaon Hotel was Dhaka's first and only five-star hotel. The lobby was modern and sleek in muted tones of grey and beige with the staff wearing beautiful silk saris or tailored suits. We walked through the stylishly decorated lobby to the café, and it too was modern, clean, and fresh-looking.

There we were, Madam Downstairs and Madam Upstairs enjoying a real cappuccino and a chat in the most unlikely place in the world. I ordered eggs Benedict, and that's exactly what it tasted like, with freshly made hollandaise sauce and Canadian bacon. Several of the colleagues I had met the night before were there and stopped by our table to greet us. I guess this was the place to gather if you wanted a break from the American Club.

When we returned home in mid-afternoon, Eve asked me to stop by her apartment around six for a drink before she and her friends left to dinner. I agreed but needed to rest for a few hours in my vast, quiet apartment that was beginning to feel like a refuge from the noise and chaos of the streets.

* * *

The music from Eve's apartment floated up to me from her balcony below as I dressed. Francis opened the door, and I was welcomed to the lovely sound of Ella Fitzgerald. Eve introduced me to her friends, and we settled into comfortable conversation. Her apartment was a fantasy land for me and a feast for my eyes. I looked around and could figure out quickly enough where her previous assignments had been. She had magnificent, large Persian carpets, several of them in different tribal styles, colors, and patterns. Similar to Ellen's house, Eve also had many beautiful Russian icons hung on the wall. Her furniture was just like mine except for a few pieces she had custom-made during her travels around the world.

I was introduced to Bob, an American engineer working on a massive rural electrification project. He was one of a large population of American engineers in Dhaka working on a rural electrification project in the countryside. It was part of a financial aid package partially funded by USAID (the United States Agency for International Development). To explain it simply, American companies bid for the project and were then paid by the U.S. government. In other words, financial aid didn't mean that we packed up a box of currency and mailed it to Bangladesh. If the projects overseas were funded by the United States, the project had to be completed by an American company and supervised by Americans. Hence, foreign aid projects benefited both countries.

As I entered the room, Bob was just telling a story of his encounter a few days before. As he was relaxing in his bed reading, he noticed something move out of the corner of his eye. When he turned his head to look, he saw a long black snake crawling out of his toilet. They all laughed at his story. I didn't. When it was time for them to leave for dinner, I excused myself and returned to my apartment. I decided to keep all my apartment lights on for the third night.

# Chapter Six

## Embassy Wallah-First Day of Work

### Sunday

The snake coming out of the toilet was the final straw. I decided that I couldn't stay in Dhaka. I would not stay in Dhaka and would leave. I arrived early to work on that first day, going directly to the Human Resource Office.

As I walked into the office, Nancy stood up and came over to me. We shook hands.

"You must be Margaret."

She asked me how I was doing, and I burst into tears. Right on cue.

"I can't do this. I can't do this," I repeated. I shook my head back and forth as tears streaked my face. I continued, "If I have to stay here one more day, they'll have to carry me out in a box."

I was determined. My mind was made up.

"Oh!" Nancy grabbed the box of tissues on her desk and offered it to me. "I'm so sorry," she said.

I took a few tissues and blew my nose. More black stuff came out. Jeez, where on earth does all this stuff come from, I asked myself.

She continued. "Don't worry. If you want to leave, we can get you on a flight on Thursday."

What? Whew, that was easier than I thought. I'm really good at this. I congratulated myself on a stellar performance. In my mind, I was already packing.

Thursday, I thought, still talking to myself. I could manage a few days.

I was just ecstatic that she told me I could go home.

Thank you, dear Lord! It worked. I was so proud of myself. I did it. I'm on my way out of here. They'll probably send me to Rome now. After all, I speak Italian. Heck, I am Italian!

She gestured to me to sit down, pointing to the chair opposite her desk.

Nancy walked around her desk and sat down.

"It's no problem. I agree, it's a tough assignment for the first time out." She's so sweet, I thought. She opened her side drawer. As she pulled out a couple of pieces of paper, she said, "You just have to sign a few papers."

Then she said, with a smile on her sweet face and looking straight into my eyes, "You have to resign from the Foreign Service and pay back the cost of your airline ticket and the shipments of your personal effects."

Smiling, she continued, "but it's no problem at all."

"What?" I said out loud. And to myself I said, resign from the Foreign Service?

No way. After all I went through to get into the Service. Eighteen months of paperwork, the endless interviews, the investigation, and numerous vaccinations. Oh my God, and that horrible medical examination!

"WAIT!" I shouted. "Wait just a second. Are you saying if I go home, I have to resign from the Foreign Service?"

"Yes." She replied, and it was clear she meant, of course.

"And pay back all the expenses?" I asked.

"Yes." She said again, still smiling.

This was something I hadn't read in the fine print.

Ka-ching! I could hear the cash register in my head.

I was speechless. I took a deep breath and thought about it for several seconds. I am not a gambler. I said, "Let me just think about this a minute."

I slowly got up. I was in shock. For some reason, that was not the response I had expected.

I didn't say another word and left her office. It didn't take me long to calculate how much I would have to pay back. My tenants in Washington would have to leave my condo. I would have to break the lease and probably pay a fine. I would be without furniture while all my worldly belongings traveled the world at my expense. Ka-ching! And my credit card bills. Yikes! And no job!

As I walked through the halls of the embassy wishing my colleagues a good morning, I finally told myself, if all these people can do it, so can I.

And thus I began my tour of duty in Dhaka, Bangladesh. I became an embassy *wallah*, an embassy worker.

I vowed to myself that I would give it two months to feel at home here, and then I would not only survive, I would succeed.

But first I needed to have a really good cry.

And that's what I did. When I returned home that evening, I cried myself to sleep. In fact, I cried for several nights that first week.

# Chapter Seven

# Getting Down to Business

I made my decision. I would complete my tour of duty in Bangladesh and I would learn all I could about this new life I had chosen. I knew I had to pick myself up and pull myself together. I'm not one to feel sorry for myself or cry over spilled milk, so to speak. I would find a way through. I told myself I was a strong, smart woman and I could do this. I *would* do this. It was time for me to get down to business.

I continued on to my office that first day, and when I walked in, Mike and Carl greeted me. We were sitting in Mike's office talking about my duties when Audrey arrived about ten. As my office sponsor, Audrey came by to escort me through the many and varied offices of the mission, introducing me to my new colleagues. I didn't tell her that I had met with Nancy earlier that day and didn't tell her that I had tried to leave Bangladesh. I decided to keep it to myself and put on a brave face.

Audrey told me that as a new member of the embassy staff, I would need to make appointments for "Welcome Interviews" with each of the department heads. Usually it's a fifteen-minute introductory courtesy meeting. She explained that the first appointment should be with the ambassador and the second appointment with his deputy. There was a hierarchy, she explained. The third interview would have been with the director of the U.S. Agency for International Development (USAID), but she was out of town. With Bangladesh's third-world status, its AID section was larger than the State Department's division. I made the appointment for after her return. Keeping with the prescribed order, I made an appointment with the Political chief, Audrey's boss.

As we walked along the embassy corridors Audrey explained the different departments. It was so interesting that I was distracted and temporarily forgot about cockroaches and snakes. I hadn't realized that several hundred Bangladeshi employees worked at the mission. The Americans were management and supervisory, whereas the local staff performed the day-to-day tasks except for classified work. All American embassies are set up the same way on a ratio of about three or more local employees for every American. Audrey knew all the Americans and many Bangladeshi employees, introducing each by name. Everyone was friendly and welcoming.

We went to the mailroom, and I was introduced to the Bangladeshi supervisor. The mailroom was under the management of the American Foreign Service administrative officer. I had mailed several boxes to myself from Washington and learned that they had been sitting in the mailroom waiting for my arrival.

We went to the embassy cashier where I cashed a personal check and received *taka,* local Bangladesh currency. I reimbursed Audrey for the purchases I'd made in the market the first time she took me out. Was it just two days ago?

We went to the security office, where I had my identification photo taken and received an embassy badge. We also made an appointment for later the following day for a welcome meeting with the American Foreign Service security officer during which I would receive information on how to keep myself safe during my tour.

Audrey showed me where the financial office was located and told me she would help with the complicated forms that I needed to fill out for reimbursement of any personal expenses I incurred while traveling. Nearby was the travel office where I could arrange for airline tickets or visas if I wanted to visit nearby countries or travel for vacation.

We went to the health unit, and I made an appointment for my check-in interview with the embassy doctor, a retired Air Force doctor, now Foreign Service. He was at post with his wife and their five children. I would bring him my medical folder and learn how to keep myself healthy during my tour.

We walked through the consular section, the largest section in any American embassy. When I arrived at the embassy earlier that day, I had noticed a crowd of about 500 people waiting in line along the outside wall. Now I could see that the people I saw that morning were filing into the embassy one by one for the three-minute appointment with an embassy representative. They were seeking visas to visit America. There was a long bank of interview windows with mostly Bangladeshi workers. The incredible statistic was that every day the embassy was open, there would be a crowd of about 250 to 450 people and maybe even more, waiting for the three-minute interview. I learned that this was true for just about every American Embassy throughout the world. In third-world countries like Bangladesh, most would pay for a shampoo and bath and rent clean clothes, hoping to look credible enough to be issued a visa. The refusal rate was 99.9 percent. While the statistic was staggering to me, I learned that each applicant was treated with courtesy and respect.

I scheduled my first welcome appointment with the ambassador and then his deputy for later that first afternoon. The ambassador at every American Embassy is the representative of the president of the United States and the chief of the mission. The deputy chief of the mission becomes the chargé d'affaires only when the ambassador is out of the country. Daily responsibilities of the deputy include the overall management of mission operations.

The other appointments with the section heads would be after those two meetings, with the political chief next in line. His responsibilities include keeping Washington informed on the country's political developments and to actively promote U.S. interests. I also needed to make a formal welcome interview with Nancy and decided I would do that last.

Since I worked in the economic/commercial section, I had time enough to learn about the country's economic reform efforts, labor practices (including child labor), trade quotas, and the promotion of American businesses.

When I entered Nancy's office later the following day, it was as though I was meeting her for the first time. She didn't mention, and neither did I, anything about our conversation the previous morning. Instead, our brief meeting was mostly personal. She asked me the usual question of how I learned about the Foreign Service and why I joined. I asked her how long she had been in the Service and learned she'd had a long career in fabulous places. She chose Dhaka as her final tour because she wanted to save money as well as make a bit extra. Because we worked on Sundays, we received a small supplement. In addition, Bangladesh was a 20 percent hardship post, meaning we received a supplement on our base salary.

When our meeting ended, she asked if I would like to join her and a few friends at her house for dinner the following evening. She loved entertaining, and it was a lovely evening with several colleagues I had met at Ellen's house on my first day in Dhaka, just three days earlier.

* * *

My social sponsor, Diana, the American employee at the embassy who would assist me with household information to help me settle in, was the person who had set up my apartment so beautifully for my arrival. The bed was made with clean sheets and blankets, the bathroom had fresh towels, and the air conditioners and dehumidifiers were plugged in and working. Diana had also stocked my kitchen cabinets with the items from the embassy welcome kit, which contained all the items a new resident would need to live for the first month or two in a country. It consisted of sheets and pillows, towels for both bath and kitchen, dishes and utensils, cooking pans, and a coffee pot. Diana was also the one who had cooked that very nice dinner of chicken and vegetables that was ready in the refrigerator when I arrived. Thoroughly thoughtful, she also included tea, sugar, and milk.

I officially moved into my apartment after my first day of work. The welcome kit also included an ironing board, iron, and hangers. I unpacked, emptying my suitcases and storing them in one of the other bedrooms. I prepared my clothes for work, hanging them in the large wardrobes. I organized the bathroom, noticing that Diana had stocked toilet paper and tissues. Room by room, I adjusted the air conditioners to a higher temperature that suited me. I knew we had a commissary where I could purchase American products and made a list of items I would need.

I walked around my new apartment room by room, knowing I needed to feel at home but not knowing exactly how I would do that. Again, I was making lists and taking notes. Finally, I decided that there was just too much furniture. The sprawling apartment was filled with U.S. government-issued furniture. It looked like a warehouse. There must be a way to get rid of some of it, I thought.

I couldn't imagine having a sit-down dinner party for a dozen people. In addition, there were two large china cabinets and two lowboys in the dining room. The living room also had too much furniture, with its two long sofas, two love seats, four upholstered chairs, two large coffee tables, and about four occasional chairs with numerous side tables and lamps. The master bedroom had two high dressers and two smaller ones. There were three large wardrobes. Each of the two smaller guest rooms had large wardrobes, dressers, tables, and lamps.

There was a fourth bedroom with its own bathroom, and that room was filled with bamboo furniture. I felt overwhelmed with it all.

I talked with Audrey about it over lunch one day. There was an embassy warehouse managed by the general services officer, and I could return some of the furniture for storage. That left me with the decision of what to return, and Audrey offered to help.

One sunny afternoon a few days later, we sat in the enormous living room drawing pictures of how we could redesign the apartment. There was a wide foyer between the bedrooms that was within the safe haven of the apartment. The entrance had a steel-lined security door that could be bolted shut. We moved one of the love seats, a coffee table, and one of the chairs into that area and made it a quiet sitting area for me. It became the most comfortable and my favorite place to relax and read.

It took time, but over a period of a few weeks, we rearranged the apartment and bought plants. When my shipment arrived from the States three months later, I added paintings and family pictures, and the apartment felt homey to me at last.

* * *

Within a month of my arrival, it was my turn to be the social sponsor for a colleague scheduled to arrive shortly, a young woman and her 18-month-old son. She asked me to arrange for a maid and a nanny and gave me a list of items to purchase at the commissary.

Most embassies have a community liaison officer (CLO), a position generally held by the spouse of an employee. The CLO usually addresses quality-of-life issues at an embassy and provides vital information for families at post as well as resources for newcomers.

Our CLO introduced me to two Bangladeshi sisters who spoke excellent English. I decided that they were perfect as they told me they had younger siblings at home and could take care of a child. As first I couldn't tell them apart, they were so similar in looks and personalities. They were cheerful and very helpful in preparing my new colleague's home for her arrival, including a crib I secured from the warehouse.

# Chapter Eight

# Night Skies and Sacred Music

With no TV or radio at home, there was little to do except read. I had already read through the books that I brought with me and had picked up a few at the embassy. My entertainment of choice would be reading and decided I needed to be certain I would have plenty of books on hand. About nine o'clock at night my first week in Dhaka, the phone rang.

"Hi Margaret, it's Carl."

"Hi Carl. What's happening?"

I had just seen him at work a few hours earlier, but I was happy to hear his voice.

"I'm going over to the club. Come with me. I'll pick you up in twenty minutes."

"Okay!" I readily responded. "I'll be ready."

I loved that he wanted me to join him. At 46, I was twice his age, yet there was a comfortableness about him that was so attractive.

I dressed quickly and was ready when I heard the doorbell. He had hired an embassy car, and we were off to the American Club.

As we approached the club, I could see the high stone wall that I recognized from that first night. There was a group of about twenty rickshaws and their wallahs in front of the entrance, and as many beggars. We showed our ID cards and entered the world of the American Club. This time I noticed the grounds and slowly looked around.

We walked along the path beside a green, neatly trimmed lawn. There was no trash, just lots of flowers. Brightly colored zinnias looked to be a favorite. There were lawn chairs placed in groups of three or four as though waiting for a friendly conversation. We passed the bright lights of the large swimming pool, and I noticed there was a man swimming laps. I loved swimming and made a mental note that night swimming in a clean pool was available to me. Soon we reached the club and walked in.

Carl confidently joined a table of five or six colleagues, and I followed him. Some I already knew, and there were a few people I met for the first time. It was so comfortable being there, and the conversation was lively and interesting. We ordered drinks, and it was a fun and relaxing evening. After a while other people from the mission joined us. I was beginning to realize that the American Club would play a big role in my social life.

It was late when we finally left the club. I just assumed that Carl had ordered a car, but he didn't. He walked straight up to the nearest rickshaw and sat down, making room for me. Carl gestured to the wallah to drive to the corner and make a right. My first rickshaw ride.

The streets were relatively quiet with very few people walking. There were a few rickshaws riding up and down the streets ringing their bells. It sounded like music. We passed families gathered together on the sidewalk. A woman I presumed to be a mother was cooking a meal, or perhaps making tea. Some people were sleeping on collapsed cardboard boxes, their only protection from the hard earth. There were some shacks attached to high brick walls, and I could see people sleeping in them. Even the roaming dogs were sleeping in groups of five or six.

I sat back in the rickshaw enjoying the night ride, leaving the task of directing the wallah to Carl. At one point I looked up. The sight was magical, and I caught my breath. I gestured to Carl to look up. The sky was filled with millions of stars that seemed so close we could reach out and touch them. As though a scene from a Hollywood movie, the muezzins from the many mosques surrounding us began their late-night call to prayer from loudspeakers, making the night ride home a spiritual experience.

# Chapter Nine

# Sunita and Feroza

As several of my friends at the embassy predicted, it wasn't long after my arrival when I decided I needed to hire a maid. It was the start of the dry season, although we had intermittent long rainy days—not a flooding type of rain, but enough to rinse the city so the leaves sparkled again in the sunlight. The dust calmed and my nose was not as stuffed with the black soot that was in the air. I learned the soot was a result of the cooking fires. Locals used dry cow dung for fuel.

I liked when it rained. It didn't last very long, and the city smelled fresh afterward. With the weather so lovely most of the time, I kept the shutters open to catch the cool breezes coming from the screened patio off the living room. Hearing the sound of the nearby mosques calling the faithful to prayer added a musical mysticism that accompanied the sound of dozens of rickshaws traveling up and down the road ringing their bicycle bells.

One day while alone in my apartment, not long after my arrival, I noticed a white powder in the corner of the living room. Investigating, I realized it wasn't powder at all. It was kind of like suds. Then I noticed it was in several corners of the other rooms, including the dining room and kitchen, and sometimes it was between the stone floor tiles. When I asked a colleague what she thought it was, she told me it was probably mold. Her recommendation was to hire a maid.

It was something I was thinking about anyway. With the shutters open, I began to feel dirt under my feet and notice that black soot was accumulating on the furniture. I couldn't imagine washing the floors of this huge apartment myself. I asked the embassy community liaison officer (CLO) to arrange for me to interview a few maids. It really wasn't much of an interview, as most spoke just a few words of English. All of them had portfolios, loose-leaf binders with letters of recommendation from former employers.

With her guidance, I chose Sunita. She started work that very day, and I told her that her main job was to wipe down the floors with bleach and water every day. While that was the main part of her job, I quickly became accustomed to coming home from work and seeing that my breakfast dishes were washed, laundry was done, and my bed was made neatly. Having a full-time maid was the easiest thing in the world for me to get used to in Bangladesh.

Over the garage, which was separate from the main house, there was a row of four small, cinderblock rooms. Each room had a small window with no screen. A lone, dim lightbulb hung from the ceiling by a wire. Each room had a pallet large enough for a mattress, but there were no mattresses. Sunita would bring her own. There was a separate bathroom down the corridor and a separate shower. I learned that Muslims shower several times a day, at least Bangladeshi Muslims do. Sunita carried her belongings into her room the very evening she was hired. The nights had begun to get cool, so I gave her a blanket.

Sunita spoke little English and could not read or write in either language. Shopping was a problem for me to solve. Going through several magazines, I cut out pictures of different fruits and vegetables. I pasted them on a piece of paper and wrote the English words next to them, and a local colleague wrote the Bengali words. I made several copies that she could use when she shopped. Somehow, we managed to understand each other, although it seemed just barely.

A colleague gave me several homemade banana nut muffins. One morning I took one out of the refrigerator for breakfast and put it on the pilot light to warm up a bit. Just then Sunita was coming into the kitchen. Her routine was to make tea for me while I was in the shower. I asked her to put butter on it, and I rushed off to get ready for work. When I saw my tea, I realized that she had put the butter in the tea.

It was a learning experience for me. Of course locals were probably not having banana nut muffins for breakfast. I didn't know what Sunita ate for breakfast and asked her. I think she didn't understand the word breakfast. Later I learned she drank tea and ate bread. I had bought bread one day in the market, but I found a bug baked into it and never bought it again.

A few days after Sunita started working for me, I began to see a young boy of about nine playing in the driveway. Sunita's son, Rafi, joined her in her room. I didn't mind him staying with her, although it was difficult making her understand that I didn't want him in the house, and she assured me that he would not come in. Rafi attended school intermittently, as schools in Bangladesh were highly unreliable. Teachers often did not show up for work, and students would then be sent home or released to roam the streets for the day.

At Christmas time, although Sunita was Muslim, it was expected that I would give her a gift. The whole experience of having a maid was new to me, and I was making my decisions based on my Western understanding of what I knew to be an employer-employee relationship. A few years prior, my mother had gifted me a lovely white satin nightgown with a lot of lace. My mother loved lace. I did not. I would never wear it, but I brought it with me to Dhaka for some reason. I decided to give it to Sunita for Christmas along with a little money. She loved the nightgown. Not long after, I remember returning home late one evening and seeing her out chatting with the *chokidar* (gate guard) wearing the nightgown. She really liked the nightgown.

At first the arrangement was that I would pay for our chokidar to have his morning tea and bread snack. I understood that Eve would pay for the evening chokidar's tea and snack. However, I noticed little by little that the shopping money I left for Sunita was running out faster and faster. Questioning her was difficult, so I compared the amount with what Eve was paying, and clearly the amount I was paying for the chokidar was considerably more. By this time, I also learned that her English comprehension was better than I first believed, although her spoken English was poor. When I confronted her about the money, her response was confusing. I decided to wait and observe a while longer.

South Asians have beautiful hair, and Sunita's was typical. Her hair was black, wavy, and thick, and she oiled it well with a combination of castor, argon, and coconut oils. I thought it had an awful smell. One night when I went to bed, I realized that either Sunita or her son had been lying on my bed. I could smell the hair oil on my pillow. When I asked her if Rafi had been in my room, she quickly said, "No, madam." I was certain one of them was lying on my bed.

The weather during the winter months was dry and sunny with the temperature a lovely 75-80 degrees. I liked the balcony doors open so I could smell the jasmine flowers and also hear the call to prayer several times a day. With the doors open, dust and soot accumulated on the furniture. It was apparent that Sunita was not cleaning the house.

In lunchtime conversations with colleagues, I learned that the maids often tested you if they knew you had never had a maid before. Several of my colleagues told me they had to fire their first maid. I told Nancy that I was ready to fire Sunita, and she offered to help me. She told me to get enough cash so I could give her the salary she earned up to that day. Sunita was then to leave the property immediately. At first, I thought it was harsh, letting her go so abruptly. Nancy told me it had to be a fast firing and she would have to leave immediately, or she would be stealing whatever she could carry during the final days. I couldn't bear to do it. Nancy did the firing, and Sunita left that night after working for me for just two months.

* * *

Before long I began to see mold in the corners of the apartment again. I had to hire another maid. Ellen offered to send Feroza in the afternoons. Feroza was happy to get the extra money. She was lovely, too, as well as a powerhouse of energy. Her English comprehension was excellent, and her spoken word was easily understandable. She had worked for Westerners for more than 17 years and knew our customs and habits. It was again a pleasure to come home to a clean house.

Ellen left on a new assignment in late February, so I took on Feroza full time. She moved into the little room in the back.

Feroza must have observed how I made my morning tea. One morning when I got out of the shower, there was again a cup of tea on my night table. It was perfect. It was like living a dream. She easily understood that I liked to be alone on the weekends and we agreed that when I was home she would quietly come into the house and prepare her lunch in the kitchen. However, housework could only be done during the week while I was at work. When I was alone, if she cooked for me, she was to leave the house when it was time for me to eat. In my early days in Bangladesh, I noticed that Sunita and now Feroza would stand and watch me eat. Like vigilant waiters, they refreshed my water after every few sips. I stopped that habit.

In time I had learned to read Feroza's moods. There was a time when I noticed her mood was quieter than usual and she avoided looking at me. When I asked if something was disturbing her, her answer at first was that nothing was bothering her, but I was insistent.

"Feroza, I know something is disturbing you," I persisted. I wanted to know if it was something I did.

Finally she responded. "Madam, in one year, two years, you will go away. But I must live here and work." True enough, I thought. I will go along my happy way, but she must live here and earn a living. Fair enough.

"Feroza, you can trust me," I told her. "I will not tell anyone."

Apparently dear Francis who worked for Madam Downstairs was threatening Feroza with sexual blackmail. He wanted sex from her, or he would do something to get her fired. I had experienced enough sexual harassment in my life to know that it existed everywhere. Why wouldn't it be here in Bangladesh? Feroza was a beautiful woman of about 40 with lovely skin and a trim figure. She was strong and elegant.

"I will do something, but before I do anything, I will talk to you." I had no idea what I could do, but I wanted her to understand that I wouldn't do anything that might hurt her chances of working with another Western family after I left. I thought about it for a couple days. I knew I could not discuss it with Madam Downstairs. Firstly, I promised Feroza I wouldn't tell anyone and also, I knew Madam Downstairs thought Francis was a saint. She was very happy with him.

I also knew that Feroza had a husband (I don't think it was official—perhaps more of a protector) who worked as a manservant at the ambassador's residence. There was a rule that maids could not have their husbands stay with them in their sleeping quarters, but I decided these were particular circumstances.

I told Feroza that I had an idea and I thought it

would work.

"From tonight, Feroza, Mohammed is to sleep here. I will make the necessary arrangements with the security office. There will not be a problem." When I told her, she clearly understood and liked the plan. It must have been the right solution because, after a few days, relief was clearly visible on Feroza's face. Whenever I saw Mohammed at the ambassador's receptions, he would silently nod his head to me.

Arrangements regarding household staff work schedules were that they would work eight weeks and then have a week off. When it was time for Feroza to take a week off to visit her family in the south, I suggested she roast a couple little chickens to take with her and gave her extra money to get a snack on the train. Since the incident with Francis, I realized that Feroza and I had developed a bond. I viewed her differently, and I believe she saw me differently as well. We were two women on our own, working and living together, although we viewed our worlds from different perspectives.

A friend loaned me a video by a Bangladeshi director, in Bengali with English subtitles. I invited Feroza to watch it with me. She stood for a long time watching the TV and finally, after several suggestions, she sat down on the very edge of the chair. She wasn't accustomed to sitting on a chair and didn't sit back. I noticed she never quite relaxed and learned she had never watched TV or seen a movie.

I knew Feroza had a lot more energy than she utilized working for me. Sometimes I found her extra work. When colleagues told me their maids were off visiting families, I offered to send Feroza. She was happy to earn the extra money. One of my colleagues needed to hire someone to iron drapery in one of the embassy conference rooms. Again I offered to send Feroza. When she showed up at the embassy gate, I went to get her. As we stepped into the elevator to go up to the third floor and the doors closed, I could see panic on her face. She had never been in an elevator before. I started telling her that I once had a job on the 52nd floor of a building in New York. It was clear that the concept of a 52-story building was completely beyond her.

Feroza remained my maid for the remainder of my two-year tour. On the day I left Bangladesh for my new assignment, we both cried.

# Chapter Ten

# Holidays in Dhaka

Along with the cooler and dryer weather during the winter months, November and December are ball season in Dhaka and throughout the entire American Embassy community in South Asia. The first ball of the season is often in celebration of the U.S. Marine Corps birthday on November 7. That year in Dhaka, the Marine Ball celebration was scheduled for the first Friday after that date. Several U.S. Marines came from nearby missions to cover security guard duty at our embassy while our nine Marines participated in the celebration.

At that time, Marines at American missions overseas serve as the security detachment and their responsibility was to protect classified information secured within an embassy. Protection of Americans on staff and other Americans living in the country is the responsibility of the country's local police force.

While in training for my assignment at the Foreign Service Institute, it was recommended that I bring several formal dresses. I had heard about the many diplomatic receptions and was excited about this new life. One dress I chose was pale aqua silk, and I imagined myself wearing it to an elegant ball.

The Marine Ball must be held at an American-owned hotel if at all possible. In Dhaka it was the Sheraton. It was located downtown about ten minutes from the Sonargaon Hotel, and although listed as deluxe, it wasn't nearly as elegant as the Sonargaon. Audrey and I planned to go together along with two other people from the mission.

Audrey told me she had scheduled a massage for early that morning. It sounded like a great idea, and I scheduled one myself. The masseuse was a Bangladeshi woman who was a chiropractor by education but making her living as a masseuse. She had a thriving business within the expatriate community and was excellent. I felt guilty paying her the fee of just four and a half dollars. In Bangladesh currency, it was a large sum for her work. Friends told me she was the sole support of her family, and her children all attended private schools.

Earlier in the month, there had been unrest in the center of the city, so we were told to travel in embassy cars only. Many people arrived at the ball in the school buses provided by the embassy's security staff.

As Audrey and I entered the hotel and walked along the hall leading to the ballroom, we could hear the music. When we walked into the ballroom, I couldn't help but smile at the familiar faces. The welcome line consisted of all nine of our Marine security guards in full dress blues. They knew they looked handsome and stood proudly. Audrey and I walked in, and the Marine closest to the entrance handed me a perfect white rose and gave me his arm. "Good evening," he said. Whoa, I thought, so formal! I had lunch with him only the day before, and we laughed and joked together. He escorted me to my seat and returned to the door to escort the next woman. Audrey was right behind me, and the next Marine took Audrey's arm and escorted her to our table.

It was about an hour before all the guests arrived. Ambassadors with their spouses from the entire diplomatic community arrived in tuxedos and gowns. When our ambassador and his wife arrived, we all stood, as was customary. Moments later, while we were all standing, the band played the Marine Corps hymn, and our handsome young Marines marched in with flags flying. Their girlfriends at the nearby tables smiled proudly. Our ambassador gave a short speech, and then the band leader announced the opening dance. The ambassador led his wife to the dance floor. After a few minutes, my young Marine came over and asked me to dance. This was by way of welcoming everyone, but I admit I did feel special.

My first Marine Ball was everything I had dreamed a ball should be. It was elegant and formal. After that first dance, the Marines each invited their girlfriends to dance, and soon dinner was served. By about ten o'clock, after our ambassador and most of the other diplomatic representatives left, the music changed. The Marines undid the top button of their uniforms, took their girlfriends to the dance floor, and proceeded to let loose. The music was loud and electronic, and it was time for me to leave as well.

* * *

Audrey invited a group of people from the mission to have Thanksgiving dinner at her house, with a turkey and all the trimmings. Our embassy commissary made arrangements to import frozen turkeys and sweet potatoes. I believe they were ordered from our embassy in Bangkok. Her dining room table, like mine, easily accommodated the sixteen guests, and everyone brought a dish to share. We had gelatin molds, cranberry sauce, and apple and pumpkin pies. It was a feast and festive with holiday music. Audrey loved the holidays, and her house was already decorated for Christmas, with sparkling lights on her tropical houseplants.

* * *

Nancy and I had become good friends by this time, and later on Thanksgiving Day, we flew to Kathmandu for the long weekend. I had wanted to go there since seeing the movie *Indiana Jones and the Temple of Doom*. Just as I pictured it, Kathmandu was dusty, dirty reddish brown, and crowded with young trekkers. Some were actual trekkers, and some were just dressed for the part like us. We met a young Irish fellow who had been working as an engineer in Papua New Guinea and who stopped in Nepal for a few days before heading home to Ireland. The three of us split the cost of hiring a driver for the weekend.

We arranged to do a short trek to a lookout point not far from the city where we could see the highest mountain in the Himalayas. It wasn't as easy of a hike as I had hoped, and I huffed and puffed and complained the whole way up. However, we reached the top just as the sun was setting on Mount Everest, and it glowed golden. Breathtaking. We stayed for a while taking in the majesty of it all until our trusty driver arrived to drive us back to the city.

Later that day, we ate a hearty meal at K.C.'s, famous because Ernest Hemingway once ate there. It was located down a dark and dirty street in the Tamil section of the city. The restaurant was crowded with trekkers in khaki pants and climbing boots. We were escorted to a table and joined several Germans who greeted us by saying, "Namaste." I didn't know exactly what it meant, but everyone said it, and I assumed it was just a pleasant greeting.

We joined in the conversation as though we were all old friends. When we were finally served dinner, we were so hungry we didn't mind that the dinner tasted just like a Swanson's TV dinner.

Our next adventure was an elephant ride through a lush city park. The elephant was gigantic and knew exactly what to do—stand next to the staircase so we could climb high enough to get into the bucket seat on top. It was a bumpy ride, and the elephant had the worst flatulence, which sounded and felt like an earthquake rumbling through his body. Aside from the odor, we laughed a lot and had a great time.

We visited a Hindu shrine where (we were told) virgins come to pray for husbands. Not far from that shrine, there was another one where the animal statues had huge male genitals. Apparently, this is where newlyweds come to pray for sons. We also visited a Hindu temple that had rats scurrying all over the place, free range. I never learned why they had rats, I was focused on avoiding stepping on one. I loved Kathmandu. It was all I had hoped it would be, exotic and mysterious.

Returning to Dhaka, I noticed an interesting sign as we went through immigration. We were directed to the line indicated for "women and other disabled persons." I smiled to myself. I was beginning to just accept these oddities of living in Bangladesh. We showed our diplomatic passports and sailed through quickly. We had arranged for an embassy car to pick us up, and it waited for us as we exited the terminal. Compared to Nepal, Bangladesh looked and smelled clean and fresh. Was I already changing my opinion of Bangladesh?

* * *

Christmas and New Years continued with a succession of concerts, parties, and diplomatic receptions. There was the United Nations Ball, the United Kingdom Ball, and the German Unification party where they flew in a huge supply of excellent sausages and served German potato salad. The most fun was the Australian Glitter Ball where everyone wore outlandish outfits made of garish fabrics. I had my outfit made by a local tailor in the nearby shopping center. A group of people from the International Club put on the HARD Ball (Happy Assholes for Rural Development). Almost everyone in the international community attended all the events, so you saw the same people at each one. The embassy provided transportation for all these gatherings as a way of supporting the staff and for security. I was learning that Dhaka was a happening place.

A group of people from the British Embassy staged a play written by one of their officers. It was an impressive and complicated who-done-it murder mystery. Each act of the play was performed in a different location. Appetizers were served during the opening scene in one person's home. The entrée was served during Act II in a different home. Dessert was served during Act III in a third person's home. We were to remain in our characters' roles throughout the evening as we traveled from place to place. It was clever and lots of fun.

Who did it? The butler, of course!

I was busy at work and active in my social life. I was learning how to play bridge and meeting people from all over the world. To my surprise, I was settling into life in Dhaka. The weather was sublimely beautiful with brilliantly sunny days in the 80s that were dry with a gentle breeze. Flowers bloomed everywhere, and there was something hypnotic about endless green rice fields. The country was bursting with color. Street vendor displays overflowed with fresh produce. I was feeling surprisingly at home after only two months.

Dhaka was, and probably still is, a vibrant and noisy city. Rickshaw wallahs continually ringing their bells, cars honking, street vendors hawking their food and wares, dogs barking, thousands of people talking and spitting, and birds singing and shrieking. It's never quiet, except in the very early morning. I began taking tennis lessons at the American Club, which was a short bicycle ride from my house. My lesson was at six a.m. One morning during my lesson, a chicken fell from the sky. It was such a ludicrous sight that I wished my family had been there to see it. I wished I had a camera. Within moments, the vulture who dropped it returned, quickly swooped down low, picked it up, and flew away. In an instant it was over. Just one of those strange things that leave you speechless.

* * *

Bangladesh was governed by a military dictator who had deposed a democratically elected leader seven or eight years prior. Discontent with the government was beginning to show by random rioting in the downtown area. Although the demonstrations were inconsistent and not near us, our security officer imposed restrictions on our travel. We couldn't travel beyond the diplomatic areas, although we were free to walk in our neighborhoods, keeping away from the main roads and the shopping centers.

On the weekends, when the curfew periodically lifted, I could go out on my own and each time I traveled a bit farther and discovered new neighborhoods. My favorite rickshaw driver would wait for me outside my house on those weekends. I didn't know how he knew our restrictions were lifted. I accepted it as one of those Bangladeshi mysteries. He was a young boy of about thirteen or fourteen, and he had the most brilliant smile. As we approached a store, children would run over to us. They somehow knew the routine and would say, "carry person" or "protector." Sometimes I went as far as four or five miles away traveling through side streets. I walked through new shops and discovered more things to buy and foods to try. I wanted to test a new dressmaker and bought some fabric. The tailor looked at the photo I showed him and motioned that he could do it.

"No problem," he said. That seemed to be the usual answer to just about any request here.

I found a new vendor who sold frozen chickens about the size of the little hens we get in our local U.S. supermarkets now. While walking in Audrey's neighborhood of Baridhara, I noticed the home where a large group of Italian engineers lived. I had met them at one of the expat community events. They had a waist-high hedge of basil surrounding it. I stopped by one day and filled a bag. One of the residents waved at me. Apparently, I wasn't the only person who noticed the basil; several people stopped by to pick it, and were welcome.

On one of my ventures, I discovered a woman selling shelled nuts. They were small, white, and mild tasting, very similar to pinole nuts. Perfect. I decided to invite Audrey and Ellen over for dinner and a movie. Ellen's friend Francine, from the Australian High Commission, joined us. I planned to debut my new recipe, *Spaghetti a la Baridhara,* my version of pesto. It was delicious. We watched the movie *The Far Pavilions* and talked of traveling to the places in the movie.

One of my favorite events was when the representatives from the United States Information Agency, now part of the U. S. Department of State, organized a performance of Noël Coward's *Private Lives.* No costumes, it was a play-reading performed beautifully by colleagues who had obviously rehearsed. I wondered if this kind of creative entertainment was usual in the Foreign Service. I hoped so.

Dhaka had all kinds of interesting and unusual events. On a sparkling sunny day, Francine organized a British high tea on the lawn at her house. She served cucumber sandwiches and tea. One evening I organized an opera night at my house, complete with a sit-down "Italian family dinner." Ellen and my neighbor Eve often had fun bridge parties. I was beginning to love the Foreign Service life.

# Chapter Eleven

# Hartals (Strikes), Garows (Roadblocks), and Miscreants (Hoodlums)

While getting ready for work one morning, I received a message on my two-way radio that all Americans were confined to their homes. Once again there was significant unrest in the city. I spent the time organizing a few more things. I had received my air shipment from the States and spent most of the day unpacking the food I'd bought at Costco, mostly cans of whole peeled Roma tomatoes, Filippo Berio olive oil, pasta, and vacuum-packed Romano cheese.

Eve invited me for lunch. When I arrived, I could hear the sound of the opera *La Traviata*. Eve had about a thousand CDs, just about every genre of music you can imagine. We agreed that opera was our favorite. We spent a pleasant couple of hours listening to music, with me watching Eve do her needlepoint. She offered to teach me. I thought it was calming and enjoyable. She had enough supplies to open a hobby store. Her theory was that in the places she was likely to go in her career, it would not be easy to shop for entertainment.

"Best to bring your entertainment with you," she told me with a knowing smile.

She suggested I do the same if I continued in this career.

That was the one-hundred-million-dollar question. Would I continue in this career? Going through the hiring process gave me the impression that I would likely go to places like Paris, or London, or even Cairo or Tokyo. Somehow, I just hadn't considered any other places. But in a conversation I had at the Marine Corps Ball, a colleague pointed out that there was only one London, one Paris, and one Rome. Whereas, in the Foreign Service, there were many Bujumburas, Ouagadougous, and Dhakas. Ah, I thought, I have a lot to learn and a lot of thinking to do, even as I thoroughly enjoyed the job and the social life.

One major downside of the Foreign Service was that I was already feeling distant and apart from my family. My family rarely wrote, and phone calls were expensive and connection unreliable. This was before the age of cell phones and email. I kept a diary of my life and often wrote long letters home to my family and friends describing my life in detail. Yes, the social life was exciting, but I was lonely. The Foreign Service was a lonely life for me, and I missed the comfortableness of being with family and close, dear friends.

After lunch with Eve, I returned to my apartment and decided to rest. I read for the remainder of the afternoon, dozing for a while. When I awoke, I was hungry and decided to treat myself to the ingredients I had just unpacked earlier that day. I made myself a plate of spaghetti with shrimp for dinner. By this time, I learned the seafood in Bangladesh was plentiful and fresh. It was a delicious dinner.

The following day we were again under curfew, albeit limited. We could go out to visit a colleague via an embassy car, but not to the shopping centers, and there would be no walking around in the neighborhoods. Audrey and I went to Ellen's house in an embassy car. Francine, our Australian friend, had arrived earlier. We spent the entire day together, playing bridge all afternoon and into the early evening. We took a break for the dinner her maid had prepared, and then we watched a movie. Ellen, like Eve, traveled with her entertainment and had hundreds of VHS tapes. It seemed everyone in this business traveled with all manner of entertainment.

Throughout the month the riots and strikes continued. I realized I was witnessing the start of a popular revolution by the people of Bangladesh. Several deaths were reported in the local newspapers. Sometimes we worked, traveling to the embassy in secure vans. The American Embassy was a few minutes away from my house, in Baridhara just over the Gulshan Bridge. Audrey lived just down the street from the embassy. I lived on the other side of the bridge in Gulshan, just across Gulshan Lake, less than half a mile from the mission. The neighborhoods of Baridhara and Gulshan were considered diplomatic areas, and they remained relatively quiet. All the protest activity was closer to downtown, which was about forty-five minutes away. Although far from the diplomatic areas, I was advised by security that Dhaka could be a volatile city, with excitable crowds forming in a matter of minutes.

The unrest downtown intensified, and by the end of November a state of emergency was declared throughout the city. Our security officer declared total house curfew for us. General Ershad was finally arrested on December 4, 1990, and was placed under house arrest in Gulshan, just three houses down the street from where I lived. Bangladesh had no functioning government at that point, no head of state.

Our ambassador, William B. Milam, a high-ranking economist in the Department of State and a seasoned diplomat, met several times with ministers in the Bangladesh government. His influence was pivotal in the decision to select a Bangladeshi economist to be caretaker of the government until a democratic election could take place. My thought was that I was living through the pages of the *New York Times* and witnessing history. It was exciting to me and I thoroughly enjoyed reading the many reports that were forwarded to Washington. What an education I was getting!

Plans were underway for a team of people from the State Department to come to advise the Bangladesh government on how to conduct a democratic election. Since 98 percent of the population was illiterate, it was suggested that the candidates choose a symbol to represent their party. The final ballot was about 16″ x 16″ and looked like a cartoon, but it was effective. For example, there was an umbrella representing a candidate promising protection and a chaff of wheat representing a candidate offering food or prosperity. Most Bangladeshis did not have TVs or even radios since there was very limited electricity available in the country and certainly not in the rural areas and the hundreds of little villages.

The newspapers were of no help either. Candidates campaigned "soapbox style." It's easy to draw a crowd in Dhaka. The picture ballot worked perfectly. Elections took place in March 1991, and Khaleda Zia, the wife of the country's former leader, became Bangladesh's first democratically elected prime minister.

That was the first, but not the last election held in Bangladesh. As of 2019, Bangladesh is still a functioning democratic country.

* * *

One of my assignments during the first days after my arrival, was to create a list of the most prominent textile manufacturers in the city representing American clothing labels. When the city was calm and we could travel, I arranged appointments for Mike to pay courtesy calls at the factories and also investigate child labor practices. Sometimes I accompanied him and saw that the large factories were for the most part clean and airy, although many children worked in these factories, some as young as six or eight.

I learned that with the schools unreliable, it was safer for mothers to bring their children to work where they earned a bit of money. With the whole family working, one child could be selected for private school. With a woman working, she could also afford birth control, further enhancing the family's economic status. It seemed reasonable to me, although I realized that not all factories were equal in their treatment of child laborers or labor conditions.

On these lovely December days, I often took a rickshaw ride home from work or over to a nearby friend's house. I loved those rickshaw rides that were slow enough for me to enjoy the sights of the city. So many children. Beautiful children, many with cappuccino-color skin and hazel eyes. Those living life on the streets were always playing games and running. Of course, if I stopped, they would beg. It was beginning to not disturb me so much, and I didn't think about it very often.

My feelings toward those beggars with what I thought was leprosy or were severely deformed was quite different. I just couldn't be around them and shooed them away, with my feelings going from revulsion to anger to guilt in quick succession. I reasoned that I had to ignore that which I found uncomfortable or disturbing and only focus on the abundant beauty of the country.

It was winter and there were flowers everywhere and the smell of jasmine filled the air. Bougainvillea of every color was flourishing wildly everywhere you looked. The rice fields were lush green, and the vegetable stands were overflowing.

# Chapter Twelve

# Behind the Veil

Nancy enjoyed entertaining and planned several brunches and dinners at her house in those early months. She lived just a short walk away. Living and working together either made you close friends fast, or you knew quickly whom to avoid. Nancy, with her cheerful personality, was a keeper. She was a natural gardener, and her home and garden were filled with flowers. She was a wonderful gourmet cook as well. She had hired a manservant named Peter who also liked to cook. The two of them were like a longtime married couple arguing and bickering in the kitchen. Peter would insist upon using a particular spice and take the initiative to add it. Nancy would yell at him to stop, mid-movement. And so it went in hilarious fashion. Live TV.

Nancy was invited by one of her Bangladeshi employees in the human resource office to attend his wedding reception. She asked if I would like to join her. Apparently both Muslim or Hindu weddings in Bangladesh could last for two or three days. The event we attended was the dinner celebrating the religious ceremony that had taken place the day before.

There were hundreds of people gathered in the

reception hall. When we walked in, many people reacted as if celebrities had arrived. We were the only Westerners invited. The large hall was separated by a curtain, one side for women and the other for men.

The bride was late by more than an hour, and the groom, Mohammed, anxiously paced back and forth, both greeting the arriving guests and asking family members where his bride was. Every few minutes, someone told him that it would be just a few more minutes. The Bangladeshi music blasted on huge loudspeakers. It seemed like pandemonium as we waited in the women's section. It was quite some time before word spread throughout the hall that the bride was arriving. We could feel the excitement.

Finally, there she was, carried up high by her male relatives on a large, red-draped pallet trimmed with gold. She was dressed in a magnificent red sari with gold trim. Her hands and feet were heavily hennaed. She wore a large, gold bib necklace, dozens of gold bangles up both arms, and ornate gold earrings and rings. Her hair was adorned with fresh jasmine flowers, and she had a gold ring through her nose that was hooked to one of the earrings. A gold pendant was centered on her forehead just above the red bindi (dot on her forehead). She modestly drew her sari across her face when she saw all the people. I got a glimpse of her face before she covered herself. Her eyes were surrounded by painted daisies with kohl centers. As the men placed her on the high stage so everyone could see her, several young women surrounded her. Everyone in the hall gathered closer to the stage. Suddenly, she put the back of her hand to her forehead and swooned back in a faint. An older woman quickly knelt down and caught her. I'm guessing it was her mother. Several young women fanned her, and she opened her eyes again. One of the women hand-fed her a morsel of seasoned rice. Another brought a glass of water to her lips, and she took just a sip. Several minutes later, Mohammed entered the women's hall surrounded by his male relatives and friends. His dress was also elaborate, white with elegant gold trim. His headpiece was a high, open fan-shaped, white hat also trimmed in gold. When the bride saw him, she swooned again and appeared to faint in the arms of the woman seated next to her.

Soon after, for some reason, Nancy and I were directed to the men's side of the hall when dinner was being served. Neither one of us knew what was happening but followed the directions. Food was served— mutton and rice. I had already eaten it several times and found it delicious.

They filled our plates with food. We looked at each other, hesitating. We didn't have forks. One of the men nearby realized why we hesitated and asked someone next to him to find forks for us. The man quickly retreated in search of the prized forks and arrived after a long while holding the forks up in the air like a trophy so all could see his success. We ate while another man took a video of us each time we lifted a forkful of food.

We never found out why we were invited to the men's side. Perhaps they wanted to make sure everyone knew they had important people as friends.

The following day, I had a chance to tell Eve about the wedding, describing the bride swooning, which I thought was dramatic behavior. She explained to me that the reception we attended took place the day after the first wedding night. The bride is supposed to act as though she, a virgin, was ravished by her virile husband. It was all theater, and apparently they all knew their roles.

# Chapter Thirteen

# Action

CNN International was our source of world news, and it was only available at the embassy. With no televisions at home, lunchtime in the embassy cafeteria was the place to gather. The news was ominous. Iraq had invaded Kuwait, and its army was proceeding to the oil fields and ports in Saudi Arabia. President George H. W. Bush was threatening an invasion of Iraq. Local Bangladeshi newspapers, whether they were pro-West or anti-West, were filled with stories of war. The ambassador enacted the first round of evacuation, voluntary evacuation of spouses and children. There was talk of a second round, evacuation of non-essential staff.

Eating hamburgers, tuna salad sandwiches, or dhal soup, my colleagues and I gathered in the cafeteria each day to hear the news of the world. It all seemed worlds away from us in Dhaka. And then one day it wasn't.

Operation Desert Storm in the Gulf began with the United States invading Kuwait on January 17, 1991. As with several American missions located in countries with large Muslim populations, we were again under house curfew. In anticipation, we had been confined to our homes for several days leading up to that date.

On the 18th, Eve and I had planned to have lunch at my house and dinner at her house, just to break up the monotony of being confined to home. We had plenty of food, and if we needed anything, we could send our servants out to buy it. Earlier in the month, when I could get out, I had bought several little frozen chickens. I didn't eat beef, and while fish was plentiful, I only ate saltwater fish—not as easy to find since it came up to the capital from the coast about 150 miles away. The nearby rivers and streams were sewers.

Eve had given me some needlepoint supplies, and even though I was making something easy, it was clearly filled with errors. I discovered it wasn't my talent. I had sent away for a few CDs, and the music was playing when she arrived. My maid prepared lunch for us and we enjoyed the afternoon listening to music, needlepointing, and talking. By about three, we were both yawning and decided to take an afternoon nap. We planned to meet up later that evening for dinner at Eve's house.

After Eve left and Sunita was finishing cleaning up the lunch dishes, I turned off the CD player. It was a sunny, dry day, and a lovely breeze filled the living room. All my windows and doors were open to the beautiful weather and sounds of the street.

When the house was quiet and I was lying on my bed, I heard a strange sound coming from outside. I couldn't identify what it was. It sounded like waves ebbing and flowing at the beach. Of course, I knew it couldn't be that, but that's what it sounded like. It was some time, perhaps more than forty-five minutes while I was still resting on my bed, before I realized that the sound was of thousands of people shouting and that it seemed to be getting louder. Instinctively I reached for my two-way radio and turned it on. (Some colleagues kept it on all the time, but I found it a distraction.)

"The crowd is just approaching the DIT1 area and is heading in the direction of DIT2." I recognized the voice of one of our young Marines. DIT2 was no more than half a mile from my house. DIT1 was about five miles away.

I called Audrey.

"Do you know what's going on?" I asked her.

"I've been listening to the monitor for a couple hours," she said. "Where have you been?"

Here, I thought, right here. I'm right here.

"It's a protest," Audrey told me in a tone that sounded like, how could you not know?

But I knew Eve didn't have a clue either. How could we know?

"There's about 4,000 men," the Marine on the radio said. "More protesters are joining them."

"Oh my God," I said in disbelief.

I had the radio on one ear and the phone I was using to talk to Audrey on the other.

"They're talking about evacuation," Audrey said. "Margaret, I can't stay here. I have five kids," she continued.

I knew that Audrey was considered essential staff because she worked in the political section.

The crowd by this time was clearly closer, and I could hear that they were shouting something in unison, but I couldn't quite figure out what it was.

The minutes ticked by.

The Marine reported that the crowd was approaching the market center, just about a half mile from where I lived. I could almost make out what they were shouting.

"That's just down the street from me, Aud."

Suddenly I understood what the crowd was chanting, and I realized I was shaking.

"SADDAM, SADDAM"

"There's a group splitting off and taking the side road," the Marine reported.

"Employees in Gulshan should activate emergency procedures and take refuge in their safe haven."

"I'll call you back," I said to Audrey and hung up the phone.

I rushed around the house closing the windows, shutters, and drapes. I ran downstairs to make sure that the main entrance to our building was locked. I listened at Eve's door. There was no sound. Frantically, I ran upstairs again, locking the door behind me. I went into my safe haven, the little sitting room where I often read and had my morning tea. Standing in the entranceway to the three bedrooms and bathrooms, I closed the heavy steel door that separated me from the rest of the apartment. I locked it and activated the alarm, hoping I had done it correctly. There was a small balcony off that little sitting area that I never used. It was enclosed with iron bars and screening but did not have drapes or shades. Then I went into my bedroom and locked that door as well. I crouched in the middle of my bed in a fetal position, terrified. By that time, I could clearly hear the crowd chanting.

"SADDAM, SADDAM!" over and over again and

getting closer and closer.

I called Audrey back.

"Somehow I didn't plan on this when I signed up," I said to Audrey, half joking. Neither one of us was laughing though.

"The main group is following Gulshan Avenue," the Marine continued reporting.

I peeked out my bedroom window and could see a group at the end of my street walking in the direction of my house. We had a steel fence around our house and a guard at the gate. Still, I didn't feel safe. I felt alone, vulnerable, and scared out of my mind.

Audrey stayed on the phone with me, and I continued listening to the two-way radio. I closed the shutters again.

Best to stay away from the windows, I thought.

Living in the diplomatic section of the city, I knew the Dutch Embassy was just down the street from me. The former Bangladeshi military dictator was in a house next to it. Immediately next to my house on the other side was the Saudi Arabian Embassy, visible from my bedroom windows. There were no other Americans near me. Just Eve and I in the house.

"SADDAM, SADDAM!"

The mob was now passing in front of my house, and the shouting of thousands of angry men was loud and terrifying. I could hear the crowd had broken down the fence and gotten into the Saudi Embassy. I could hear yelling and crashing glass and could imagine they were rampaging through the building and destroying furniture and breaking machines. I could see the moving shadows reflected on my bedroom wall.

"A group of about 800 entered the Saudi Embassy," the marine said. "The majority of the crowd is just on the other side of the bridge heading to the embassy," he continued. Our embassy was just on the other side of that little bridge over Gulshan Lake, where the main part of the mob was obviously going.

That was the last message I heard from the Marines. The monitor went silent. I knew several Marines where disguised and embedded in the crowd on the street. After about twenty or thirty minutes there were no more sounds coming from the Saudi Embassy, and the group that had broken in was joining the main group that was crossing the bridge. They were just steps from the embassy.

The American Embassy was often called the Big Red Fort. It was a large, imposing building built of red brick and surrounded by a high brick wall and an equally high, parallel iron fence. It stood in the middle of lush rice fields and could be seen from four or five miles away over squat ramshackle buildings.

There was no gunfire. The crowd had only sticks, but several men tried to climb the fence. The nearby Bangladeshi police stood by and did nothing. Ambassador Milam was in his home several blocks away and I learned later that he called his contact in the Foreign Ministry. I understand his message was simply, "Have the police disperse the mob, or we have no choice but to call in the military." The country had just gotten rid of their military dictatorship and was not willing to take a chance on it returning to power. Truckloads of police arrived within minutes and beat back the mob with clubs, brutally whacking them.

Most of the crowd dispersed and left the area. Several hundred others began walking in the direction of the American Club. Still frozen with fear in my bedroom, I could hear the sound of the mob retreating farther and farther away. I was still holding the silent walkie-talkie in a tight grip when it suddenly came alive in my hand and startled me.

"They're heading toward the American Club," the Marine said. It was a different Marine this time. I didn't recognize his voice. I had no idea what had happened while the monitor was silent.

I learned later that a mob of about 500 did get into the American Club. They scattered, trampling flower beds, tumbling planters, and throwing lawn furniture into the swimming pool. They threw rocks, breaking most of the windows. Again, the Bangladeshi police dispersed the men, but not before they did significant damage.

Suddenly the protest was over. As quickly as it had started, there was once again calm.

Silence.

I remained in my room behind the locked doors for the remainder of the day, finally sleeping. I never went downstairs to Eve's house for dinner. When I awoke early the following morning, I was still in the clothes I had worn the previous day. I opened the security door of my safe haven and went into the kitchen to put the kettle on. My apartment was silent and somehow it felt ominous rather than secure.

I learned the mob that had gotten into the Saudi Embassy had destroyed furniture and equipment. The estimated total number of protesters was about 8,000. In talking to Eve the following day, I learned that she had instructed the guard at our gate to say we were Dutch if anyone in the crowd asked who lived in our house. I thought, that's one I have to remember.

Day-to-day life almost returned to normal. Some days we worked, and some days there was sufficient unrest in the city to warrant a curfew. It depended on how the Gulf War was going. Audrey, as she was considered essential, worked most days. I worked in the economic/commercial section of the embassy. There were no calls from American companies wanting to do business in Bangladesh.

Audrey never mentioned the protest, and neither did I, as much as I wanted to or needed to. The days continued to go by in a steady stream of blazing sun, cool evenings, and small gatherings with different colleagues close by. Life was more than bearable. Life was pleasant again.

But the terror of that day never left me. January 18, 1991.

* * *

When I returned to work on January 22nd, I took my turn on the "rumor control desk" for a couple hours. The consular section had the phone number of every American in Bangladesh if they had registered with the embassy. I called each of the people and read the statement prepared by the ambassador giving them information on the stability of the country and the status of the Gulf War. Although the embassy had evacuated spouses and children earlier in the month, many of the Americans in the country did not leave but rather kept a low profile. Many of them were representatives of nongovernment agencies, American contractors, and numerous religious organizations.

# Chapter Fourteen

# Super Cyclonic Storm BOB 01

The Gulf War officially ended on April 11, 1991. The diplomatic areas of Gulshan and Baridhara were calm again, and life in Bangladesh returned to usual after the Gulf War—sunny days, joyful children, and busy markets. The local English-language newspapers had many stories of "miscreants" causing trouble in the different areas of Dhaka, but for the most part, we were again free to roam the city.

Sadly, and not unusual, the local papers also had several stories every day of young brides who perished when their saris "accidentally" caught fire while cooking, or they unknowingly drank poisonous substances. Many Bangladeshi marriages were arranged with the bride's parents paying a dowry to the groom's parents. The bride would then go to live in the home of the groom's mother. In the poorer communities, it wasn't uncommon for the bride to be killed by the groom's family so he could remarry and collect another dowry. I learned about this practice in the United Nation's Human Rights reports.

The weather was changing again. Most days it was sunny and hot, but it was unmistakable each day that the humidity was rising. The dehumidifiers scattered around my grand apartment were working overtime and overflowing. Feroza kept busy emptying them.

Leaving the house one morning, I noticed a strong odor of garbage. It was overpowering and nauseating. What could it be? I searched and soon learned what it was when I heard a ripe durian fruit crash down from a nearby tree and split open on impact. I had noticed the big brown pods on the tree but kept forgetting to ask what they were. Colleagues told me they tasted delicious, but I could never get past the smell.

As another sign of the change in weather, I began to see bubbles in my apartment walls. The high humidity caused the mold in the plaster to grow, bubble out, and eventually crack through the paint. I first noticed this strange occurrence in Eve's apartment. It had been only a year since the walls in her apartment were repaired, and now they were due for repair again. It wasn't long before I received a notice from the general service office that my walls were scheduled for repair in September.

During this time of renewed normalcy, the ambassador held a "lessons learned" meeting with each of the department heads about what worked and what didn't work on that January day at the start of the war. These meetings with the ambassador, deputy chief of the mission, and the department heads or U.S. government agencies were generally called "country team" meetings. Sometimes I was chosen to take notes. One of the most interesting tasks of my job was to cover meetings, taking notes for colleagues not in the meeting. It was a good way to learn what each of the departments focused on day to day.

The participants came up with a list of immediate requirements. One was to restore a previous procedure that required each office to have no more than two hours of destroy time for classified documents in their safes. This State Department rule was already in place, although it had not been strictly followed. It would be now. Each office was required to reduce their stored classified documents to a maximum destroy time of two hours.

We chose April 29, 1991, as the day we would do the time-consuming and messy job of cleaning out our files. The plan was that we would start early in the day to shred the documents and finish the job by evening. We planned to have dinner together afterward at a nearby *dhaba*, a neighborhood restaurant.

There were two small windows in my office, and to me they were like movie screens. I could watch life in Dhaka go by, and it was forever fascinating to me. I remember the weather throughout the week was strange, with pale lavender-grey skies. It was the beginning of the rainy season, my first rainy season, and when it rained in Bangladesh it poured. Within minutes, there would be streams down the street. Within an hour, streets would be flooded, and the locals would seek higher ground, often sitting on top of their roofs or anyone's roof. So many people lived on the streets, I couldn't even imagine where they all went.

The rain would start with big swollen raindrops falling intermittently, hitting the ground with audible plops. Then, within minutes it would come down in sheets, a drenching soaking rain. I don't recall it ever just sprinkling.

That morning, I didn't wait for the embassy shuttle van to pick me up. I hopped a rickshaw and arrived at the office before anyone else. I was sorting through the large safes in our office as my colleagues arrived. We worked nonstop throughout the day, taking only a short lunch break. The sturdy commercial-sized shredder in the office filled bags and bags with shredded paper, which would be sold to local recycling plants after it was mixed with shred from other offices.

We finished shredding just after six. I was covered in dust from the shredding, and I know I smelled, but we all did. Exhausted, we closed the office and headed to dinner. There were only four people in our economic/commercial section of the embassy, and I had nicknames for everyone, including myself. I thought of Mike as Chief Perry White. I called Carl Jimmy because I recall Jimmy Olsen in the old TV series, Superman, because Jimmy always wore a bow tie and Carl often did as well. Chris—our new, young, gorgeous junior officer who had arrived just a month prior—was Clark. Guess who I was? Yep, I was Lois.

Mike and Carl drove to the restaurant together, and I drove with Chris in his new car, an ancient army jeep. I noticed it was oddly quiet with few people on the streets, although the rain had stopped earlier in the day. The restaurant was empty as well for some reason. Granted, six thirty was early for Bangladeshi dinner. We ate our dinner with the usual good humor and jokes. I really enjoyed my colleagues and loved the job, too. It was perfect harmony. We laughed a lot.

When we left the restaurant, Chris and I talked about how beautiful the sky looked. It was dark grey by this time, still with that lovely light purple tint. It was after eight, and the wind had picked up, swirling debris in little twisters. The quiet was unsettling. There were no barking dogs roaming the streets, no beggars, and eerily enough, no birds chirping. Although strangely quiet, it was lovely. It was close to nine when Chris dropped me off at my house.

I woke up at about eleven thirty that night to the sound of slamming shutters and rattling windows. Looking out my window, I noticed that a sheet-metal roof had blown off a nearby shack and was barreling down the street. There were more swirls of rubbish and then suddenly the sound of a loud cracking. A large tree limb had snapped off and fallen across the road. It was clearly a storm, and the noises kept me awake most of the night.

On the way to the office the next morning, I saw that there were many trees down blocking the roads. Several of the flimsy houses along Lake Gulshan had collapsed and had been windswept into the lake.

My colleagues who were on the shuttle bus with me talked about the several tornadoes that had hit the city. So that's what it was, I thought. I could see the streets were swept clean as though a giant broom had come in and pushed everything—shacks and trash into Gulshan Lake.

When we arrived at the embassy, we heard that a major cyclone hit the coast in Chittagong, 150 miles south. The statistics came in throughout the day, and the numbers were staggering. The estimate was that 138,000 people and 200,000 animals had been washed away into the Bay of Bengal by 15-foot tidal waves. There was a 20-

foot storm surge with winds up to 160 miles per hour. Small fishing boats, as well as large tankers, capsized and sank, clogging the entrance to the major port.

When the storm was over, thousands of bodies, both human and animal, lay dead along the extensive coastline with few people alive to claim them. Food and crops were destroyed, and the ramshackle houses were blown away. The Indian Meteorological Department gave it the technical name of Super Cyclonic Storm BOB01. It was the deadliest tropical storm on record at the time, and it left a trail of devastation on a massive scale.

Many survivors, after drinking contaminated water, had diarrhea as well as respiratory and urinary tract infections, and scabies was common. Within days, the rotting bodies caused the first signs of typhoid fever and cholera.

With the Gulf War over, President George H. W. Bush directed the USS *Tarawa* troop and supply carrier to stop in Bangladesh on its way home from the Persian Gulf to provide humanitarian aid. Initially 3,400 Marines landed in Chittagong under the command of General Henry Stackpole. A local English-language newspaper quoted him saying that, "We went to Kuwait in the name of liberty, and we've come to Bangladesh in the name of humanity."

Within twenty-four hours, the U.S. Marines from the *Tarawa* set up water purification stations, medical care facilities, and MRE (meals ready to eat) distribution centers. It was an incredible organizational accomplishment to witness. A local citizen called the Amphibious Task Force (ATF), "Angels from the Sea."

The U.S. government called it Operation Sea Angel, one of the largest military relief operations ever undertaken.

International news organizations sent reporters to Dhaka. American military helicopters from the aircraft carrier were provided to survey the damage, and smaller U.S. military aircrafts were flying in and out of Dhaka airport, using the embassy as a base of coordination. The military established an amazing satellite communications network. The ambassador's conference room was turned into the military headquarters in Dhaka.

The embassy went into high gear. I was working in the ambassador's office in twelve-hour shifts to cover the workload. In the middle of an incredible amount of stress, confusion, and workload, I received a call from an American newspaper reporter who was hoping to get the first photos, stating that, "My mortgage and the education of my children depend on me being on one of those helicopters." He was hoping for a scoop.

One of the local anti-American newspapers reported that the American military had invaded Bangladesh to establish a new base on the South Asia coast because they had been thrown out of Subic Bay in the Philippines. In response, the U.S. Army sent a team of lawyers and conflict resolution experts from Okinawa to speak to the Bangladesh government.

After several high ministerial meetings, a document was drawn up, typed by Audrey, declaring that the humanitarian aid operation would last exactly forty-five days. At that time, all American military would leave Bangladesh. The documents were drawn up, and arrangements were made for a formal signing ceremony.

I had some red ribbon and got two large gold stars from the local American school. The documents were embossed with the great seal of the U.S. Department of State.

The ceremony took place at the Bangladesh Foreign Ministry. One signed document was given to the Bangladesh foreign minister, and the other was given to the American ambassador. I believe it's in the National Archives in Washington, D.C.

Operation Sea Angel ended on June 13, 1991. All of the military personnel that had participated in the rescue effort left Bangladesh as agreed upon forty-five days after the signing of the agreement. The ambassador's conference room returned to a conference room, and country team meetings resumed as usual.

I was awarded a Meritorious Honor Award along with several of the embassy staff.

# Chapter Fifteen

# Day by Day

## Summer 1991

The Bangladesh government stabilized after the election of its new prime minister in March of that year. Begum Khaleda Zia was the spouse of a former president. Her only true rival was Sheikh Hasina, the daughter of Zia's husband's political opponent. Politically the government settled into its routine. The streets were calm, and there were no more curfews. Few areas of the city remained off limits to us or were considered a risk. I traveled throughout Dhaka city, visited the Hindu and Buddhist temples that I wanted to see, and toured the more rural areas around Dhaka. Many days I just stayed close to home and shopped at the two nearby shopping areas. The shop owners and vendors knew me. The beggars knew me, and my entourage of children knew me. I was in my neighborhood and went about my business.

The long rainy season had begun, and it was just that, rainy and blessedly quiet. It dragged on with a soaking rain each day, as predictable as the day itself. Sometimes it rained for only an hour at a time, and sometimes it rained for an entire day. There were stories of rats climbing up into the trees to avoid the snakes that had been flooded out of their nests. Luckily, for me the stories of rats and snakes remained just that—stories, although I did check my toilet regularly.

To me the rain was always refreshing, and I never minded the way it left the air smelling clean, washing away the dust on the trees and filling Gulshan Lake. The rice fields were being planted all around Gulshan and Baridhara, and I anticipated them bursting bright green in a month or two.

Work returned to its routine pace as well. By this time, I knew just about everyone in the mission by name. My job was somewhat interesting yet not extraordinarily exciting or challenging, although I enjoyed reading the many political and public affairs reports that were cabled to Washington. Also, it was hectic and varied in that I never knew what to expect. We colleagues often shared information, and it was endlessly interesting to hear about each other's work and, I suppose, to learn the local gossip. A young family left suddenly because the woman jogged in shorts and t-shirt, entirely inappropriate for a Muslim country. She refused to change her outfit or stop jogging. Not wanting to risk a riot, the ambassador asked the family to leave. It wasn't a request.

I began to think about my next assignment. In a couple months, I would begin the bidding process. We in the Foreign Service begin considering transfer about a year before the actual date. I had not yet made my decision on whether the Foreign Service was for me although I was leaning toward a career.

Summertime was also a series of Hail and Farewell receptions as many people transferred out of the mission and new people arrived. Nancy retired and left post.

Eve's career also came to end, and she returned to her little cottage in California. Ellen had transferred to Bangkok a few months earlier. A new ambassador's secretary arrived who had formerly worked for Ambassador Milam in Washington. Jennifer was smart and always had time to help. She was a welcome addition to the embassy. She arrived with her two handsome high-school aged sons, both becoming basketball legends in the local American Overseas School.

There were other occurrences as well that seemed bizarre to me and yet I could say I saw it with my own eyes. At the American Club one day I met a couple, two young people in their mid-to-late twenties. They were impersonators. The young woman was blond, but that was her only resemblance to the singer Madonna. The young man had dark brown hair that he wore piled high on top of his head. He obviously used a lot of lacquer because when the wind blew, his hair didn't move. He was the Elvis impersonator. The theatrical agency they worked for in California booked them on a South Asia tour, but unfortunately it went bankrupt and the two performers were stranded in Bangladesh. Hopefully, the American Citizen Services representative in the consular section of the embassy helped them. Unfortunately, I never did see their act.

An American country-music singer came through, quite a good singer, too. His performance was at a local hall. The theater was filled to capacity with mostly Bangladeshi young people. It was so unusual to attend a live performance that we gave the singer a rousing round of applause. As I recall, he was the only performer who came to Dhaka during my tour, except, of course, the Madonna and Elvis impersonators.

There were tragic stories as well. One in particular was a young American woman of about sixteen or seventeen who was caught at the Dhaka airport trying to smuggle several large bags of cocaine or heroin out of the country. She had them taped to her body. This was before the days of X-ray machines, but she was caught anyway. The penalty for drug smuggling in Bangladesh at the time was death by hanging. Somehow our ambassador was able to convince the government to spare her because she was a minor. I recall she was sentenced to life in a Bangladesh prison. Some twelve years later, I learned from a colleague that she was exchanged for a Bangladeshi prisoner we had incarcerated in the United States.

There were a couple of local English-language newspapers. The stories in them were often just as strange or ridiculous. A man was arrested robbing a store; he was caught with the evidence, a pocketful of chocolate.

And so the summer passed, and it was time for me to take my one-month vacation. I planned to travel to Italy where I would meet my parents at the apartment they usually rented on the beach in the little town of Scauri, just south of Rome. My father had a big family in Scauri and the surrounding countryside called Marina di Minturno. I looked forward to the familiarity of the village and lazy days on the Mediterranean beach. I often met family members on the beach or at the local markets.

I flew into Rome, and on the taxi ride from the airport to the train station, the city felt familiar. Even when the driver drove up a one-way street to avoid traffic, it didn't bother me at all. On the train from Rome, I wasn't at all surprised to find a seat on the train opposite cousins. We talked of family, and it made the hour and a half journey fly by. They drove me to the beach house. With no phones at the beach, I surprised my parents. They knew I was coming, but I hadn't informed them of the exact day of my arrival. It was a joyous reunion after not seeing them for a year. I wore the gold pants and tunic top, salwar kameez, that I had bought on that first day in Dhaka with Audrey. Within an hour, I was sitting on the beach with my mother, talking as we both watched my father dig for *tellini* (tiny shellfish) at the water's edge. Later that day, my mother made a light red tomato sauce with them and served them with spaghetti.

The month flew by, and I returned to Dhaka feeling relaxed and refreshed. While I was gone, the city had bloomed, and on the drive from the airport, I could see field after field of lush green rice well on its way to harvest. Workmen had repaired the walls of my apartment, and Feroza had cleaned after the extensive work was completed. Everything was pristine and I was happy to see her, and surprisingly, I was happy to be home. Yes, I was home.

I returned to work with renewed interest in my job and happy to see my colleagues. After the teasing comments about "life on the Riviera," it was work as usual. In the pile of mail waiting for me was the bid list from Washington, the list of open assignments in the Foreign Service. The complicated bidding process had begun. It would be months before I would learn where my next assignment was. There was no doubt in my mind that I would continue in the Foreign Service. I made my decision based on age and finances. At almost fifty, I decided I was working for a secure retirement. The Foreign Service would give me that.

# Chapter Sixteen

# Lily of the Field

Early November 1991

The phone beside my bed had stopped working, so when the call came in from my Australian friend Louise, I had to race across the apartment to answer it. The distant squealing woke me from a deep sleep. I finally picked up the receiver on the fifth ring.

"Hello!" I said, out of breath and still groggy.

"Hey Margaret. I've been trying to call you. Where were you last night?"

I ignored the question.

"Louise. What's going on? It's so early." The sun was just coming up.

"Margaret, you have to come over now. You're not going to believe this."

Louise told me that a homeless woman had given birth to a baby in the open field next to her house.

"What?"

"Margaret, she doesn't want the baby."

This young girl, we learned, had come to the capital from a village in the south to earn money to send home. She was about sixteen years old when she found herself alone, pregnant, and living on the streets.

Dhaka's streets teemed with homeless or near homeless people. Even in the so-called diplomatic quarter, people set up shelters made of cardboard boxes, dry palm fronds picked up from the street, or if the person was lucky enough, some pressed board discarded by an expatriate. Or, more often than not, people just slept on the street. The air was dusty with ash from the cooking fires of dry cow dung, as millions of Bangladeshis lived life on the street.

I was riding a bicycle in those days and quickly dressed and rode over to Louise's house. Her maid, Shefele, expected me and showed me to Louise's suite. There in the middle of her bed was the most perfect little baby girl. I picked her up in my arms and had the immediate thought that she was mine.

"You have to take her, Margaret. You told me that you had always wanted a child. Here's your chance."

Louise went on and on.

"I can't have a baby with my lifestyle," she said. "And anyway, you know the ambassador likes you. He can help you get her out of the country."

Louise was right about her lifestyle. She traveled throughout the country often.

This was the clincher. "I named her Lily because she was born in a field."

Louise was an Australian woman who was assigned to Dhaka years before to oversee the clothing production for a major textile manufacturer. The agreement was that she would stay for two weeks maximum. But now this was perhaps her eighth or ninth year, and she owned two or three clothing factories here and lived quite the charmed life of a rich foreigner.

Louise went on to tell me the story. She had returned from work about six o'clock the night before. As she was pulling into her driveway, she saw a large crowd of men huddled in a circle in the field next to her house. She told her driver, Robin, to go and see what was going on. He reported that a woman had given birth and that there was a lot of blood.

"The woman is dying," he said.

"Bring the baby to me and take the woman to the maid's quarters," she instructed him. "Tell Shefele to give her some tea and bread. She's probably just starving."

Louise took the baby, covered in dirt and afterbirth, and gingerly carried her to her room. She washed her in the sink with perfumed soap and wrapped her in one of her old pink t-shirts. Afterward, she told Shefele to go to the market and buy a baby bottle. Then she called her doctor. He immediately came to the house and saw to it that the mother was cared for with appropriate medication. She had not passed the afterbirth. He then examined the child and declared her a full-term, healthy baby. After a bath and some food, the woman fell asleep, exhausted. She never asked after her child.

I recalled that Audrey was planning a trip to the commissary later that day. I suggested we give her a list of needed items. Louise and I agreed that we couldn't trust buying formula on the local market and knew that disposable diapers were impossible to find in Bangladesh. We felt like two conspirators planning a great international kidnapping.

When Audrey heard the story of Lily, she said she would come over immediately. Sure enough, super-efficient and take-charge, Audrey arrived within about a half hour. She had raised five children by herself and knew a lot about babies and their care. She scooped Lily up in her arms and held her so lovingly. I recall feeling jealous. She looked so confident in holding the baby. In return, Lily gurgled and farted.

After just a few minutes, Audrey said she thought Lily peed. I took Lily in my arms and put her down on the bed, thinking I would change the toilet tissue I put between her legs. Instead of urine, she released the meconium in my hand. Somehow, I wasn't repulsed by catching her first bowel movement. I felt so much love for this lost child. Yes, I thought, I will take Lily. I carefully washed her and put some flowery smelling talc on her and finally added fresh toilet paper between her legs. We began to write a list.

By about nine thirty in the morning, Lily had had quite enough sugar water and began to wail. We took turns carrying her back and forth and rocking her in the hopes of soothing her. Poor baby, her face turned magenta with sobbing. It would be another three hours before the commissary opened, and it was easily an hour's drive away. I didn't know what to do, and neither did Louise. We looked to Audrey. We had told her earlier that the mother was still sleeping in the maid's quarters. Audrey told us to have the mother breast feed Lily. Although reluctantly, I gave Lily to Shefele to bring to her mother.

She returned a few minutes later with Lily still wailing loudly. By this time Lily's face was deep purple, and her screams were so pitiful. Shefele told us that the mother said she didn't have any milk.

Audrey again took charge, although I could hear my silent voice yelling, "NO!"

"Shefele, put Lily to the mother's breast and force her. The sucking motion will start the flow of milk," Audrey said authoritatively.

* * *

I didn't stay long at Louise's house that day. I left and rode my bike along the side streets. I recall I cried when I returned to my apartment, letting this incredible wave of sadness wash over me. I must have cried for a long while and awoke later in the day to the sound of the muezzin's call to prayer. I thought back over the day.

* * *

Shefele returned after about an hour. Alone.

We all looked at her with a puzzled expression, but I believe we all knew what had happened. Once the mother breastfed Lily, she couldn't give her up. It took the mother just a few minutes to disappear into the crowded streets of Dhaka with its millions of homeless.

I never saw Lily again.

Louise told me that a few months later, the young mother came to her door wanting to sell Lily. Louise gave her a bit of money with the hope that she would use it to buy a train ticket back to her family in the village. Perhaps she did, or perhaps she found someone to buy Lily.

# Chapter Seventeen

# On the Job

As the months passed, my acquaintances widened to include people from other embassies as well as people who were working on various government projects. I realized I lived in a world set apart from Bangladesh, yet in the heart of the capital. As I was to discover through the years, my "culture" remained the same wherever I was posted. This is the dichotomy of the Foreign Service. We live in a foreign country, but we are clearly not of that country and we are looked upon as the foreigners we are. This was clear to me when on several occasions when I invited a few Bangladeshi colleagues to have lunch at my house. I realized the conversation was guarded and barely relaxed. This was disappointing to me, although I did have the privilege of enjoying many social occasions with Bangladeshis.

Millions of dollars were pouring into Bangladesh in the form of foreign aid for redevelopment projects. There were representatives from Japan, and for a while I taught English to their wives. They wanted to learn American English. I met the secretary to the Embassy of the Holy See, a religious sister from an order that provided Vatican embassies worldwide with office support.

My circle of friends was varied, and my social life

was active. I often socialized with my Bangladeshi colleagues and enjoyed many invitations to their home. Although they were not always comfortable and relaxed when visiting my home, they were gracious hosts and made me feel comfortable when I visited them. They also knew the best places to shop and where to find the best prices, and they kindly shared that information. I was learning about their culture and they were generous in explaining their customs. When I was invited to a celebration at a Pakistani friend's home, I bought a beautiful gold silk sari. Two colleagues came to my house around eight to dress me for the event and taught me how to wear it.

I was comfortable not accepting every single invitation I received from my American colleagues, as I had when I first arrived. Diplomatic reception invitations from the ambassador were required attendance. I had to work. We were expected to arrive ten minutes before the start of the reception, which was usually the hours of seven to nine p.m. A colleague briefed me on what to do. Greet the guests upon arrival and steer them in the direction of the bar and food tables. Our job was to mingle with the guests during the reception. At about eight forty-five we were to steer the guests toward the exit. When all the guests departed, we could go home. It was fun for the first two or three diplomatic receptions.

* * *

Increased stability in the country meant the commercial/economic section was busy, and I found the work exciting and interesting. Representatives from the French government won the contract for installing telephone poles. However, we Americans won the contract for the telephone wiring and we were already working on a massive rural electrification project. Bangladesh was being transformed, and I was witnessing it.

One day in the office, I received a call from a businessman in Iowa who owned a factory that produced bridge kits, similar, I imagined, to the erector sets of years ago, like the one that had been my brother's favorite toy. These bridges in a kit could be assembled in a few weeks by a small crew using the simple directions. They could be disassembled and moved as well. In a delta country like Bangladesh, they would be invaluable. The representative sent me the sales kit, which our office presented to the Foreign Ministry and we also kept a copy in the Commercial Library.

Biman, the national airline, was looking to expand their local service. There were teams of engineers building airports throughout the country, and Biman was negotiating a purchase of small secondhand jets from McDonnell Douglas Corporation. The job of our office was to facilitate the American companies in meeting and negotiating with the Bangladesh government's economic/commercial section.

A group of people from our embassy were invited to visit a new ceramic factory funded by the Chinese government. We were shown the entire factory, from the mixing of the ceramic to the mold to the decoration of the dinnerware. Hundreds of people were employed in a modern assembly line factory. We were offered an irresistible discount, and we all bought full sets of beautifully patterned dinnerware.

We visited a boarding school for homeless young

girls run by the Salesian Sisters, an offshoot of the Sisters of St. Francis de Sales. These young girls lived at the school, attended classes, and were also instructed in making the most beautiful fine embroidery. The school supported itself by selling the linens. Of course, many of us ordered table linen sets. I ordered a tablecloth with twelve matching napkins designed with a cluster of grapes—not inexpensive but perfectly created.

The clothing and textile manufacturing business in Bangladesh was expanding rapidly. Factories were springing up every week, and there were jobs for women. Usually women didn't work, but with the growth of the clothing manufacturing industry, there were numerous jobs available. For months my colleague Carl had been working with the manufacturers of red shop towels, the towels most often used in gas stations. The manufacturers of these shop towels in the United States had been lobbying the State Department, complaining that the Bangladesh manufacturers were overproducing, not honoring their trade quota agreement, and flooding the U.S. market with the cheaper product. U.S. manufacturers of shop towels hired a lobbyist to advocate for them, which eventually reached our office, declaring a protest in the form of a diplomatic note, which our office delivered to the Foreign Ministry. This objection by the U.S. manufacturers would continue for my entire tour of duty without a resolution. The Bangladesh government simply ignored it. As I understood it, they would ignore it until they could upgrade the shop rag factory into a clothing manufacturing factory.

Just as I had promised myself on that day so long

ago when I tried to resign, I had settled into my life in Dhaka, occupying my time pretty much doing what I had been doing in the States: seeing the latest films just as soon as we received them, reading a wide variety of books and sharing them with colleagues, shopping in the local stores, and often cooking for friends. I enjoyed the company of many friends, both in my embassy and from foreign missions.

In time I learned about foreign affairs, trade quotas, labor laws, and reciprocity laws. Experiencing the world from this perspective, living in a foreign land, and meeting the people was all endlessly interesting to me. I had made the right decision in joining the Foreign Service, albeit impulsively. I believe that I was fortunate to experience life here.

Life was good, and I was happy. I was well into my second year. If I thought about it as two years, the time seemed overwhelming to me. Taking it one day at a time seemed the way to accept my life here. There were times when I felt completely overcome with fatigue and more than once I was certain I had caught a terrible disease—and it wasn't always a false alarm. Once it was a rather nasty case of dengue hemorrhagic fever, a disease spread by mosquitos.

On a few occasions I picked up a case of giardia, an intestinal infection caused by feces in my food supply. The high fevers, diarrhea, etc. didn't last long, and Feroza became not just my maid, but on occasion, my nurse. I went to our embassy doctor, and usually one injection did the trick, clearing it up in a few days. And then there were times when I went to the doctor in tears with complaints of not being able to sleep. Although a medical doctor, Dr. Yun had vast experience in the third world and would often explain culture shock to me and its physical effects. I would come away renewed and able to face another day.

I recalled a comment made to me while I was in training at the Foreign Service Institute in Washington. "Take plenty of books with you because nothing ever happens in Bangladesh." I learned that was a completely untrue statement. Since arriving more than a year and a half ago, I had witnessed strikes, violent demonstrations, a political coup, a popular rebellion, a mob attack, tornados, a killer cyclone, pestilence, extreme poverty, constant harassment by deformed and sickly beggars, disease, and an all-out U.S. military emergency relief effort.

I had dealt with a new country, new city, new job, new friends, new house, new food—and still I survived. And something else happened along the way, something quite interesting and unexpected. I fell in love with Bangladesh and all things South Asian. Yes, I suspect it was the people, the lush countryside, and what remained of the British architecture. Bangladeshis are friendly and gentle in manner, and the history and culture was infinitely interesting to me. Above all, it was the children that totally enchanted me with their beautiful bronze faces and playful personalities.

# Chapter Eighteen

# South Asia Daze

When I returned to Bangladesh from my trip to Italy in early October, I could tell that the weather had changed again. The dehumidifiers throughout my house no longer overflowed. The sun was at a different angle, and a sliver of bright light peeked through my bedroom shutters each morning. I was able to open all the windows and balcony doors and enjoy the gentle breezes of the season.

Audrey told me she was planning a trip to India in April, to visit all the places in the movie we saw together, *The Far Pavilions*. Audrey would plan the whole thing. I didn't realize she had watched the film several times and made notes of all the places. Ellen would fly from Bangkok, and we would all meet in Delhi.

Up to that point I had traveled to Calcutta several times for brief weekend getaways. Calcutta was a shopper's paradise with beautiful deluxe hotels and excellent food. I enjoyed the magnificent architecture left by the British. I could only imagine what I would see and what I could buy in Delhi and beyond.

My travels had taken me to Bangkok for a long weekend and to Nepal with Nancy that first

Thanksgiving. I got to see the top of Mount Everest at sunset, albeit from a distance. I enjoyed traveling to the northern countryside of Bangladesh and visited several tea plantations. Traveling through India's Rajasthan, land of the kings, sounded like the perfect way to wrap up my tour of Bangladesh.

* * *

Early on a Friday morning the first week I was back from Italy, I was feeling like I had returned home after a long absence. I was enjoying sitting in the large area between the bedrooms, my favorite and most comfortable place to sit and relax in my cavernous apartment. Feroza made me a cup of tea. I often had my morning tea there and read whatever newspapers I had collected or whatever friends had passed along to me during the week. It was my private time.

I was happy yet didn't know why, except that I was looking forward to visiting the local shopping center. I hadn't been there since returning from Italy and would enjoy seeing all my "friends." What treasures would I find today?

I dressed quickly, left the house about ten o'clock, and walked in the direction of the local market. The usual entourage of barefoot children followed me, and I smiled and laughed at their happy faces. They knew I would buy ice cream for them after I shopped. Joining us were several rickshaw wallahs who were hoping I would get tired and hire them. And, of course, there was the familiar band of beggars. Somehow it didn't disturb me seeing them that morning. As I walked along the street, it always amazed me how many men asked me if I wanted my shoes shined. I was wearing rubber flip-flops.

I realized the beggars, the men peeing on the street, and the red phlegm everywhere didn't bother me anymore. When I first arrived, it disgusted me. From that reaction, I went to anger. The people irritated me, and sometimes I growled at them or shoved them away. Then I felt so overwhelmed with guilt followed by anger toward myself for being so cruel. I went through the period of oblivion. I didn't see them. I just ignored them. Now as I walked, I realized that I had just accepted it as Bangladesh and frankly was grateful…there but for the grace of God. I was often filled with gratitude for the many opportunities I enjoyed by the circumstance of my birth. Throughout my time in Bangladesh, my emotions remained raw.

At the shopping area I negotiated for a carry-person and a protector, and I knew that several other children would join us. It was a way for them to earn a bit of money, as I usually gave all the children a few taka, Bangladesh currency.

I wished I knew the names of these beautiful children who made a living for their families on the streets. There was this little girl of about seven, covered in dirt and with matted hair and rotten teeth. I think she fancied me her friend. I suppose I fancied her my child and sometimes felt overwhelmed with love for her. Then I saw another child that I knew, a charming little boy from the neighborhood with a dazzling smile. He stood a bit back until I designated him to be my protector. All together now, we entered the shopping area, me and my entourage.

The children gathered around me, knowing I expected them to keep the beggars at a distance. I had already gone through the panic stage with the embassy doctor when I thought I had tuberculosis or leprosy.

I often wrote home to family and friends telling them about the bounty of fresh fruit and vegetables, and often they wrote back wondering why there was so much poverty in the country. My only answer, whether right or wrong, was simply too many people. Birth control was difficult to come by and costly. Feroza told me she took birth control pills but that they were quite expensive.

I went upstairs to the antique shops with my entourage. Although the children and beggars followed me, they were not allowed into the shops up there and waited outside. My favorites were the antique brass and furniture shops. I could browse leisurely, looking at all the amazing treasures.

It was the ball season again, and I stopped at the fabric store. The Australian High Commission was planning their annual Glitter Ball. I planned to get a sparkling new Indian outfit. It was so much fun designing my own clothes.

When I finished shopping, I asked another child to find me a rickshaw while I bought about a dozen ice cream pops from the local vendor. These kids knew my routine and politely waited for their treat. There was one woman who always followed me, and as much as I tried to ignore her, she would push her way in, so I couldn't avoid seeing her grotesquely deformed face just inches from mine. Once I pushed her away so hard she stumbled and looked at me with an expression that I interpreted as, "How could you be so cruel?" I felt cruel, too. I asked myself, "What have you done? What have I become? Margaret, pull yourself together." I felt so guilty afterwards that I gave her some taka and an ice cream pop as well. I remember the incident as though it took place yesterday. It still haunts me.

* * *

I looked forward to stopping at my Australian friend Louise's house for a light lunch before returning home. It was nice to see Louise again and so refreshing to have a friend who was not part of the embassy staff. I trusted her discretion, and she was comfortable talking with me. At my age, Louise had lived in New York for several years. We had much in common. We ate in her lovely sitting room filled with fresh flowers from her garden and listened to classical music. We talked about the people we knew and caught up on local gossip. I left her house about two in the afternoon after a delicious lunch of cool shrimp salad and iced mint tea.

Outside every expatriate's house in Dhaka, there were usually a half dozen rickshaw wallahs waiting for passengers. I chose one that I knew. My very own chauffeur, I smiled to myself. He was only about thirteen or fourteen years old, I think. Who can tell the age of people? I knew he worked hard every day. Probably he supported his widowed mother. That was the usual story. We took off. I didn't have to give him my address. He knew where I lived. They all did. I imagined these poor street people knew everything about us, the foreigners in their midst.

It was one of those radiantly sunny October afternoons. He took my favorite back roads, avoiding the wide thoroughfares and traffic. It was hot and dry, and it seemed the whole world was sleeping. I was looking forward to a nap myself. Even the birds were napping as we rode along the silent streets. We turned a corner, and stretching before us was a long alleyway with high, red-brick walls on either side. It was silent except for the almost indistinguishable squeak of the rickshaw wheels and the ringing of bells. I dreamily looked ahead and saw that the overgrown bougainvillea trees on the large estates cascaded over the walls, crawling to their kind across the way. Long stretches of bright red, violet, pink, and white—lush and endless.

Way ahead, I noticed a lone figure slowly walking toward us. I couldn't tell what or who it was from the distance, but some minutes later she slowly came into focus. A young girl, perhaps about ten or twelve years old, strolled along the road. I could see now that she was barefoot and dressed in a brown, soiled dress that was in tatters. She was talking to herself and moving her arms gracefully. I could see that she was immersed in her imaginary world.

Closer now, I could see her features. She had that cappuccino-colored skin that I loved so much about the Bangladeshis. No blemishes marred her face. But what most impressed me was her posture. She walked as though she was wearing a crown. It would have seemed perfectly natural had she nodded to her citizenry and waved.

As we passed each other, we smiled and she flashed her eyes, which were intensely green. Strangely, I'm not sure she actually saw me, she was that absorbed in her fantasy. As we passed each other I looked back. Her hair was heavily oiled and braided into a thick rope that hung down her back to her waist. I don't think I had ever seen a more beautiful child.

# Chapter Nineteen

# Arrivederci

My second holiday season in Dhaka passed in the usual stream of Halloween costume parties, elegant balls, and Christmas concerts. The weather was dry and the days sunny, with the daytime temperature in the low eighties. The steamy hot days of summer were over. Rice fields were lush and the produce stands overflowing.

In March Audrey received word that her next assignment was to the United Nations delegation in Brussels. She was excited to get a European assignment and planned to travel to Bangkok to have several tailored business suits made. In Thailand she would have a choice of better-quality fabrics. One by one my colleagues who were scheduled to rotate out during the upcoming summer months learned where they were being assigned. There was some excitement, some relief, and some disappointment. Rome was my first choice, but I was told it was a long shot to get such a plum assignment so early in one's career.

In April Audrey and I traveled to India, first taking a short flight to Calcutta. From there we boarded the Rajdhani Express, an ancient train left over from the days of the British Raj. The journey from Calcutta across India to Delhi would take about seventeen hours. The porters proudly wore the old colorful uniform of that era, although they were frayed at the cuffs and significantly faded. Our train car was surprisingly air conditioned, and the service included meals. I couldn't imagine how they cooked the food, or under what conditions, but decided to forget about cleanliness and just enjoy the scenes of rural India that we observed through our picture window.

I never did learn how Audrey managed to make all the reservations. This was before personal email, and there were few fax machines. But somehow she did. When we arrived in Delhi, we had a car waiting for us. The terminal had thousands of people, and yet we found the young man holding a little sign with Audrey's name. Incredible!

There was a saying in the Foreign Service that went something like this: Foreign Service secretaries were "faster than a speeding bullet, etc." Corny, I know, but I did learn that if you want a job done well, ask a Foreign Service secretary to do it. We were highly trained, masterfully efficient, and incredibly reliable. We had a stellar reputation, and it was well earned.

Ellen was already there when Audrey and I arrived at Ellen's friend's house. She was the Foreign Service nurse assigned to our embassy in New Delhi. We toured Delhi for several days before leaving on our week of traveling through Rajasthan. Audrey had arranged for a car and driver. The car was reliable and the driver amicable, although I'm not sure he understood much English. We had reservations at maharajah palaces and hunting lodges all through the "land of the kings." We visited all the forts and monuments we remembered seeing in the film. When we arrived in Agra, we had just enough time to see the sun setting on the magnificent Taj Mahal, breathtakingly beautiful with its white marble roof glowing in the sunset. It was equally extraordinary the following morning when we took our time and visited the tombs of both emperor Shah Jahan and his favorite wife, Mumtaz Mahal.

Each day we toured and shopped throughout our travels. Our routine was to meet in the evenings in the lobby of our hotel wearing whatever we had purchased that day. One night when I was the last to arrive in the lounge, I noticed an interesting looking man sitting off to the side. His hands were in the yoga position, and I realized he wasn't sleeping, he was meditating. He was dressed in a long, dark green, velvet robe, completely inappropriate for the weather. He wore a sparkling silver turban, fastened on top with a large red jewel. A long white feather was stuck in top that finished off his impressive outfit. The sign next to him simply said, "Fortune teller."

Intrigued, I approached him and asked if he would tell my fortune.

"Of course, Madam." He motioned for me to sit.

He went on to tell me a whole monologue of ridiculous things as I sat there listening to him, enraptured by his accent and soft voice. Then he said, "You must always wear smoky topaz jewels. It is good luck for you."

"Oh, well, then I guess I must buy myself some smoky topaz," I responded with a smile.

"I just happen to have this ring that is smoky topaz."

I bought it, although skeptical that it was real. But I love the story, and it continues to be a favorite ring.

It was a magnificent vacation, and I vowed one day to return to India. As luck would have it, I've had the opportunity to make several more visits. But I will never forget that memorable first visit. Shoppers let loose in the shopper's paradise called India. After our incredible ten-day tour, we flew from Delhi to Dhaka loaded down with carpets, clothes, and jewelry. It was wonderful.

Within a couple days of returning to Dhaka, while at home one evening, I received a phone call from the State Department. My human resource officer in Washington informed me that my next assignment was chosen. When I was a young girl on my first visit to Rome, I had a wish that one day I would return to live there, visit all the museums, and drive to the hundreds of small hilltop villages.

To my delight and astonishment, my dream was coming true—I was advised my next assignment would be secretary to the American ambassador in Rome, Italy.

# About the Author

# In Her Own Words

I never considered myself adventurous. I just had this extraordinary curiosity about "the other" side of the world, the people who lived there and how they lived. I could read about them, but I wanted to see for myself. Fortunately, I was hired for my first airline job at 21, and soon after that began to see the world. After about thirteen years and the deregulation of the industry, travel was much more difficult with fewer flights having seats available for non-paying travelers.

I missed traveling, but wasn't unhappy. I had a good job in the defense industry. I had also begun taking classes at the local community college, finally getting my high school diploma. Yes, I was a high school dropout.

I was 44 years old with only an Associate's Degree when I learned about the Foreign Service. I applied and passed the tests to be hired as a secretary. I had challenging assignments and plum assignments. I lived in Dhaka, Rome, Havana, and Ashgabat, as well as traveling to Moscow, New Delhi, Mumbai, and the United Nations as part of the Secretary of State's diplomatic detail.

Each time I returned to the States to take a Washington assignment, I enrolled in school, finally getting my Master's Degree at 63. I loved school and loved my job.

Hellen Keller was right. "Life is either a daring adventure or nothing." I just preferred the former.

*Margaret Riccardelli*

# ACKNOWLEGMENTS

To my dear sister Connie, all my love and gratitude. I will always remember you presenting me with my letters, tied with a ribbon, when I returned from Bangladesh. You smiled and said, "Here's your book." And indeed, many of the stories came from those letters.

Sincere appreciation to Gail Spilsbury, my friend and noted writer, whom I met in Rome as part of her writer's group. We faithfully met every Tuesday evening in my apartment and shared our poetry, children's stories, screenplays, and short stories. Your steadfast encouragement and support have made this journey possible.

Appreciation to Dr. Edward Jones, my professor and mentor at George Mason University. Thank you for your guidance and inspiration.

Big thank you to Sr. Vita Marie, my sister who believes in me unflinchingly. Shout out to Mary Ann, my sister who believes I can do anything.

With gratitude to my friends Susan Weber, Eileen, and Tonia Decosimo. My friends who patiently read my drafts and offered appreciated critique, thank you.

## If you enjoyed this book...

Please leave a review and let others know.

•••

**Learn more about Margaret and her adventures. Follow “Margaret Riccardelli Author” on Facebook**